Ms Kel

CAPTAIN COMMUNICATOR

How To Turn Signals Into Superpowers

Breathe Fire

Blaise Hunt

Blaise the Trail inc.

Blaise HUNTER ®

Team Lexi

CAPTAIN COMMUNICATOR

Tellwell Talent
www.tellwell.ca

ISBN
978-0-2288-6424-0 (Paperback)
978-0-2288-6425-7 (eBook)

DEDICATION

This is for all the haters, critics, oppressors, and trauma. You tried to silence me but instead you strengthened me. Without you, I would never have written this book, pursued my healing, or chased my destiny with such relentlessness and a resolute spirit. Thank you for provoking me into my purpose. You were always part of the plan. You have been my greatest teachers for I am unchained because of you. Our foes are the key to our freedom.

TABLE OF CONTENTS

PROLOGUE

Wouldn't it be amazing if we could go anywhere in the world and be marvelous interpreters? Every day we miscommunicate, whether to ourselves or to others. Our world is filled with signals and messages. How good are you at sending and receiving them? Do they get lost in translation? Would you like communication superpowers? Even though superheroes are fictional, humans have an inner fantasy of being a secret spy and possessing superhuman abilities. If you could be any superhero, who would you be?

How many people said themselves?

If you aren't a superhero in your mind, you won't be one in life. Tapping into the communication superpower begins with how we allow our minds to communicate to us. This drives how we see the world and how we choose to transmit messages. We can't effectively send and receive messages with others until we master our own communications system. Language contributes to our well-being, and the well-being of those around us. Are your inward and outward signals the hero or the villain in your story? I am a communications expert by trade and yet throughout my life, I was a horrible communicator. Through trauma, hardships, conflict, loss, breakdowns, and bounce backs, I discovered the key to effectively communicating is through human connection. Our life experiences, environment, and genetics contribute to our comms systems becoming vastly disconnected. The connection within determines how our internal and external transmitters will operate. Once we re-establish healthy lines with ourselves, we can learn how to communicate like a superhero and be a universal translator.

How do you define communication? Why do you think we have so few communication skills in a communications-obsessed culture? What does your self-talk look like? Do you have an inner dialogue? Are you constantly facing mixed messages and conflict because everyone seems to be on a different frequency? Join me on this journey of exploring various areas of our lives that are suffering all because of a lack of empowering communication. There are millions of books on this subject, but *Captain Communicator* takes a daring approach. Each chapter focuses on a specific topic that humans encounter daily. I weave my own story of ups and downs and show how we can connect the severed lines to become the hero of our signals instead of the victim. Even though we all have unique life encounters, we all require the same communication skills to thrive not just survive.

After going through earth-shattering traumas and developing a rare autoimmune disease, I was forced to make a choice. Either I stay the course and die—or face the mirror, rewire, and live. These words make up my life. I invite you in to see all the good, the bad, and the ugly. Through it all, we can obtain tools to navigate through life in a brave way. A hero's journey isn't about the wins; it's about how we take the losses and turn them into life-giving superpowers. Authentic communication, heroic honesty, unique observations, risky perspectives, and courageous self-reflection fill each page. This is my medicinal manifesto. I wrote this book because I refuse to wither and die emotionally, spiritually, and physically. Disease, miscarriages, trauma, pain, and heartache don't define me. By reconnecting the portals of communication, I starve this disease and inject healing. This is for me and for you. Let's be Captain Communicators together and run this world.

Love, Blaise

CHAPTER

1

KNOW THYSELF

FALSE IDENTITY

True communication requires authenticity. However, we live in a world full of illusions and aliases. How many versions do we have of ourselves? We have our social media self—showcasing all the wins and accomplishments but not the losses. We have our professional self—pursuing validation, promotion, and success while never exposing untidy emotion. We are trained to be cutthroat and robotic. Status, money, power, and belonging determine the costumes we put on. Impressions mean everything and fuel the narrative for the need of masquerades. Somehow, we have bought into the idea that our raw authentic selves are not worthy of display. We mask, we hide, we manipulate, we add filters, we show parts but not all, and we carry multiple emotional passports with us every single day. We have our parent persona in front of our kids. We are one way with our partners and another way with our friends. We have our sport selves, and we have our dignified church selves. We are just characters we play and depending on the audience, we act accordingly. Who are we? Unpacking this question activates communication in the purest form.

Taking on a false identity in real life is much different than in the movies. We are not James Bond, nor do we have alluring disguises or collections of passports with exotic names. Humans often have an inner fantasy to be a spy, superhero, or jewel thief. These pursuits are sensationalized in any superhero box office hit. In real life though, the disguises we apply to cope and escape aren't sexy or glamorous. We continue with the facade because we don't believe our honest mortal selves can be cast as the hero in our story. Our culture teaches us that vulnerability is weakness. We reward fake perfection and punish messy authenticity. I am a quick study: the moment I experienced a communication breakdown, I realized applying phony masks provided me with a sense of strength and control. Armour is thought to be a positive thing. The better the armour, the better the protection. However, the opposite is needed for the human spirit to flourish. In our world, the concept of removing protection to build strength is bizarre. Since it is human instinct to want to have some control, defenses play a huge part in the quest for safety and dominance. I didn't grasp the power of vulnerability until my late thirties, so I had many aliases to sift through to find myself. My masks started off as coping mechanisms but over time they hurt me more than helped.

The problem with relying on masks to endure issues is the line soon blurs between our true nature and that of the alias. The two bleed together and we are left feeling like an imposter in our own life. The ancient quote "Know Thyself"[1] resonates with me as one of the most profound statements of all time. Everything we think, say, or do is all connected to how well or little we know ourselves. We are told to love ourselves and to own who we are, but we can't truly know ourselves if we are constantly judging, questioning, or hiding our true nature. This establishes an identity crisis. How can we work through circumstances, traumas, and challenges if we don't know what we need to solve them? We tell people to have positive mental health and we link it to having good self-esteem, but is that the right approach? I believe that the key to unmasking and solving the identity crisis plaguing humankind is found through achieving self-respect.

I'm here to open the dialogue about people respecting themselves throughout their life. Having solid self-respect is essential to being a strong communicator, and we can't expect others to respect us if we don't respect ourselves. Self-care, self-love, self-confidence, and self-worth are all buzz words, and we go rah-rah about them. But if we don't reconcile those values with the ultimate goal of self-respect then we are willing participants in our identity theft. We need to stop the repetitive cycle of using an alias to manage hardships and challenging situations. We need to strip away the layers of masks and aim for a communication reboot instead of adding more firewalls. That will save us from the in-house burglary. If we are all walking around with fake identities trying to survive our lives, the concept of "know thyself" will remain foreign. Yet, knowing ourselves is the linchpin to our internal and external communication signals. If we don't discover the truth of our soul code, we will continue to have crossed wires and miscommunication.

Connection is the purpose of all communication. The intention with this book is three-fold: to reconnect my body with true acceptance and health, to inspire healing in others, and to connect to my father's heart. I am forever grateful he is still in my life and stayed in the game. Dad, you are my hero. Your competitiveness and drive are in my blood. You are worthy. You belong. You are accepted. I love you with all my heart.

"We are sorry, but we presume your dad dead." That one sentence cut the communication feed within me and changed the course of my entire life. I frequently have flashbacks to standing in my grandmother's condo complex. We had been herded in like cattle waiting to be slaughtered with devastating news. That memory still brings me to tears at the drop of a hat. The family was all huddled together and two police officers stood in the middle. After two days of dragging the river, there was still no sign of life, just an empty red canoe. We had all known the outcome in the back of our minds, but for some reason hearing it verbalized took us out at the knees. Everyone was sobbing, yet it was also eerily quiet. The silent shock was deafening. I could not accept what I was hearing. The only way I could communicate that refusal was to let out a blood-curdling scream, "NOOOOOOOOOOOOOOOOOOOO!" I think I repeated it over and over. After the fourth time, others began to wail in response to my grief. My mind, body, and soul couldn't comprehend what was happening or what was to come next. So, all three collectively decided to cut all transmission to protect me. For the next fourteen years, I lived in total darkness. A literal human shutdown. I was alive and acted somewhat "normally," but I had completely disconnected from myself and from my misery. This life-altering trauma triggered me to commit my first fraud. I took on an alias and actively participated in my own identity theft for years to come.

Careers and relationships were my accomplices. I could hide in them. As a chameleon, I was good at being whatever people needed me to be. I became a news reporter because I love to ask questions and get to the heart of every story. It was also a way to morph into another identity. It was like the reverse of Clark Kent—it was my disguise that gave me superpowers. In the newsroom I was taught to ask the five Ws in all my interviews—Who, What, Where, When, and Why. Years later, as I embarked on my journey to restore the lost signals within, I realized the same interview strategy could be applied to my personal life. I was lost in the maze of masks, but I knew deep down there was a woman I could love and adore. Discovering my real identity was the key to restoring healthy communication again. So, I tweaked the five Ws and created an identity checklist to help me find my way back.

- Who am I?
- What makes me unique?
- Why am I here?
- Where do I want to go?
- When is the right time?

I run through this identity check every single day. My identity faces challenges all the time not only from my own fears and thoughts, but also from other people. Yet if I don't know who I am, where I am going, or my why, then I can't stand in my power because I don't know who I am contending for. And it's impossible to respect something you do not know.

ME, MYSELF, AND I

Communication is a three-way street, yet it all boils down to respect. We can't effectively send and receive messages with others until we master our own communications system. The core of all exchanges needs to come from self-respect. Practicing a clean internal dialogue leads to an "environmentally friendly" communication model inside and out. So how does one build self-respect? What helped me was going through the identity checklist I just mentioned and committing to owning who I am, flaws and all. I relate it to going through a "soul scan."

When we travel, we willingly submit ourselves to the metal detectors and x-rays because we want to get on that plane. We need to have that same resolve with surrendering to our own internal scans. This detection system is essential to understanding who we are so that we may take steps to honour our identity. That is self-respect in a nutshell. Humans often shy away from these internal snapshots because it is uncomfortable to look at ourselves fully exposed. It's like the elephant in the room. We all know what's hiding beneath the surface but if we don't acknowledge it, somehow it doesn't exist. What does your self-talk process look like? If you were to hold the scan results up to the light, would they be clear or polluted? We often don't pay much attention to what we are thinking or saying to ourselves, but this inner monologue is crucial. It all comes down to knowing and respecting "me, myself, and I." If we evade the regular scans and checkups, we are in essence disrespecting ourselves. Respect stops the identity mugging.

Once we get in the habit of respecting ourselves, we begin to learn who we are. So, when people or circumstances challenge our identity or our beliefs, we have the tools to express who we are from an authentic and loving place. I like to compare this practice to facing customs agents. I had an incredible opportunity to live in the UK and travel all around Europe right before the pandemic. From venturing to Ireland to kiss the Blarney Stone, to walking the cobbled streets of Montmartre in Paris, to being awestruck by the mysteries of Stonehenge, I earned pages of stamps in my passport.

Earlier I mentioned committing identity fraud, but that was metaphorically speaking. I have a clean record. But why is it that you always feel like you are a criminal when you wait in that line and face the firing squad at customs? I was travelling with my six-year-old daughter at the time and because of child trafficking, I was always grilled a little more than others. Proof of school enrollment and financial records were always requested. Then they would ask her if I was her mom. She would stare at the officers blankly and was too intimidated to answer. I was screaming in my head, "OMG, say I'm your mom!" After a while I was always let through, but in those moments of being questioned, my heart pounded and

I felt like I should confess to something. Those interrogations made me question my own identity and innocence. I feel like this happens beyond the border crossings, as if we are constantly facing customs agents in our lives, and they are scanning us. Who are you? Are you what you say? Does your story check out? We must create an internal passport for ourselves just like our travel documents. Believe it or not, one is made whether you create it intentionally or not. If you don't, the "internal passport" goes to default mode and becomes a false identity. Then you really are an imposter in your own life. So, it all boils down to the Identity Check. If you build your own internal passport and stamp it each day, you will boost your confidence because you will have built your own identity—and you have the passport to prove it.

The biggest adversary to identity comes from a virus in the communications system: negative self-talk. We usually engage in this when we feel triggered in some way. What is a trigger? It is a physical or emotional reaction that activates our sympathetic nervous system—fight, flight, freeze, or fawn. We can't self-regulate in that defensive mode. We need to get into the offensive position. So, part of self-respect is learning how to transition from the reactive "danger alert" state into the calm "rest and digest" state, controlled by our parasympathetic nervous system. This allows us to step back and create a courtroom in our minds to weigh the evidence and take conscious action rather than simply react. We need to get real with ourselves and admit what those triggers are so we can identify them right when they happen. *This* is self-regulation and that's achieving a deep respect for yourself.

When something triggers me, I get heart palpitations and I get extremely hot. My ears burn like wildfire, and panic ensues. My go-to response would be to flight, freeze, or fawn. I recognize this was coming from that protection/reaction mode rather than from a critical thinking and action mode. Now I wait until I achieve a more rest and digest state before responding. We are notorious for creating a storyline in our heads to justify our emotions surrounding an issue. The stories we tell ourselves when we are in trigger mode are usually pure fiction. When we buy into the plot, that narrative becomes our reality. We then continue writing fiction and sell it to ourselves as a true story. This is negative self-talk. Recognizing my triggers and what causes them helps me stop the mixed signals. It's like defragging my computer, and it creates clear pathways to communicate with others more effectively, efficiently, and positively. So often, we are just reacting to each other's triggers which causes more code to unravel and creates a perpetual cycle of miscommunication.

DON'T LIE TO ME

We must protect the purpose of communication—connection. Have you ever woken up feeling like you could conquer the world but throughout the day "customs agents" started popping up, challenging your very worth and identity? If we don't learn how to deal with those so-called agents, whether they are our own toxic thoughts or another's comments or behaviours, we can end up beaten down and lost. So how do we preserve the purpose of our exchanges? This is where the self-regulator comes into play. We are our own greatest BS detector, but only if we allow ourselves to get that honest. No one else can do it for us. To ensure I'm being honest with myself, I ask, "How much I want to respect myself today?" Only an answer of pure truth is acceptable. I must steer clear of faulty reasoning or justification for my actions, and of accepting toxic thoughts as reality. By tuning in to a deception alert and building a filtration system or mental courtroom, I can allow the good thoughts to flow in and the bad to be sifted out. To learn self-regulation, you might ask such questions as:

- Is this true?
- Is this just my defense mechanism?
- How can I neutralize this?
- What can I do in this moment to de-escalate?
- What appropriate action can I take that doesn't have me buying into these negative thoughts or storylines?
- Can I shift my perspective and see this from a different angle?

Sometimes it's as simple as admitting *I don't know how to deal with this thought or issue right now. I give myself permission to shelve it temporarily, gather more intel, and exit the situation until I can make an accurate decision.* Did you see what I did there? I didn't become a victim of my thoughts. I took ownership of them and guided myself through a series of questions back to a rest and digest state. Tackling negative self-talk is just about practising being the ruler of our thoughts; there are good ones and bad ones, and we are the masters of them all. This incredibly empowering shift is the beginning of developing a profound respect for yourself because you now know thyself.

BODY LANGUAGE

"You have an autoimmune disease, where your body physically attacks itself? Do you think there's a link with your condition and how much you hate yourself and how you attack yourself everyday with your thoughts?" This was said to me at my very first appointment with a BodyTalk practitioner. Those two questions transformed my life. At that moment, I stripped away the aliases and dedicated myself to connection through vulnerable and candid communication. To know ourselves, we must learn how to interpret what our bodies are trying to tell us each moment of every day. Our bodies consist of a highly intelligent major integrated communication network, sending and receiving messages on a continual basis. Our bodies are somewhat like computers, and we should treat them with the same care as we do our smartphones and laptops. When's the last time you recharged your body battery? Have you ever installed an internal firewall? How often are you doing updates? Do you do regular defrags and resets, or are you just waiting until your body has a complete crash? We must start examining our bodies and giving them more respect than what we have in the past. Without properly functioning bodies, we begin our days with bad signals and are vulnerable to deadly viruses.

Since 2005, I have battled a rare autoimmune disease called EGPA, formally known as Churg-Strauss syndrome.

My body is constantly sending mixed signals which causes one giant system breakdown. The medical system isn't designed to find the source of the problem, but rather to treat the symptom. BodyTalk gave me the tools to help decode my own body and sent me on a quest to learn how to speak my body's language.

A disconnect between body, mind, and soul creates portholes for bad reception and lost signals. We need to link them together again, so they work for us not against us. We do this by understanding the true function of our body and how it is designed to operate. Did you know our emotions govern our organs? According to Traditional Chinese Medicine, each emotion correlates with a specific organ in the body. We experience numerous feelings and emotions in a day, but do we ever wonder where they go after we encounter them? I find it fascinating that we all feel the same emotions in our lives no matter who we are or where we are in this world. Our emotions are a universal language. Through connecting feelings to organs, we have achieved a breakthrough in decoding signals.

Let's examine some of the main emotions and their associated organs. Researchers have found anger and jealousy rule the liver. Joy and hate influence the heart. Fear affects the kidneys, ears, and bladder. Grief and depression sit in the lungs and skin. Worry and anxiety manipulate the spleen, stomach, and pancreas. The large intestine is a reservoir for sadness, grief, and fear. With this insight, I was able to investigate what is at the root of EGPA for my body. I deal with a variety of symptoms but the main one is debilitating asthma, which affects the lungs. From there I discovered an avenue to pursue—grief. These findings put much into perspective. I became my own private investigator looking for clues and connections. When you sit back and look at yourself or others and their ailments, this new method really makes sense. You can see the illness and how it links to those exact organs and emotions. When I found out lung issues really mean a grief issue I knew I had to face an ugly truth—my past trauma. That is another thing that is universal. Trauma affects every person on this earth without discrimination.

When we feel sorrow, grief, or depression it generally means we have experienced a deep pain physically or emotionally. After dealing with a life-threatening illness for many years, I went on a crusade to find a way to heal. It took a visit with a naturopath for me to discover the connection between the illness and my unresolved grief. She had asked me point blank if I had experienced any grief in my life, and it was there in a little room that I finally revealed my true identity. I spoke for the very first time of all the tragedies I had experienced in my life. I listed off how my house burned to the ground when I was in grade twelve. The structure and security of my life became unhinged; my home was not safe anymore. A couple years later, a devastating break-up left my heart shattered into a million pieces. That heartbreak opened the door to some other horrible boyfriends who abused me mentally, physically, and emotionally. I felt worthless and rejected. Then after all that came the biggest pain of all—abandonment from my father. For years, I had never processed any of those traumas. Yet in that moment with the naturopath—a lady I had never met before—I had an epiphany, and tears flooded from me. You see, asthma correlates with un-cried tears[2]. I was literally choking on my own sobs and suffocating on past hurts. Finally, I began to listen to what my body was trying to tell me.

I was all in from that point. My investigation led me to clues and discoveries about myself. I took courses and became certified in various holistic healing modalities. I learned that everything is connected. We can't isolate one symptom or one traumatic event. They all link to each other. Consider the term *disease*—a lack of ease happening within. We need to connect the dots and commit to creating ease in our lives. To do this, we must understand where the communication gaps are and devote ourselves to bridging them. I shared how our emotions govern our organs, but did you know the body also has three brains?

When we speak of a brain, we usually are referring to our head brain, but there is more to consider when speaking about the brains of the body. We have the head brain which is basically an information processor. Signals get transported to the mind and then we translate, process, and spit out an action code. In recent years, scientists have discovered there is a heart brain and a gut brain as well. The heart is responsible for love, harmony, and creative thought and sends more information to the head brain than vice versa. The gut brain oversees not only digestive information, but also joy, drive, and purpose. Often, we talk about dopamine and serotonin levels and associate them with our minds, but in fact those two things aren't massively produced in the head brain at all. Over 95 percent of serotonin is generated in the gut[3] and 90 percent of dopamine stems from the heart brain[4]. If we have a communication breakdown in any of those brains, we are in *dis-ease*. When one of those intelligent systems is even slightly off, nothing will speak the same language. How can we expect to send and receive clear messages with others if our own bodies are experiencing shutdowns and are unable to transmit messages within itself? To be a Captain Communicator, we must learn the language of our bodies.

360 SCAN

How often do we stand in front of the mirror totally naked and scrutinize ourselves? When facing the looking glass, we tend to dismiss or quickly glaze over our perceived flaws and only focus on what we can tolerate. The internal scan is just as scary. Seeing ourselves from all angles and various perspectives is difficult. There's no hiding from anything. Even if we are familiar with our weaknesses or wounds, we often conceal or deny them to avoid being accountable for them. We choose ignorance over awareness. But to fully optimize communication within ourselves, we need this complete view before we can possibly know where to zoom in—or where to concentrate our efforts. By first zooming out, we can discover where the fogginess is obscuring reality. How distorted or choppy is the frequency? This helps us sift through false filters and get to the true likeness. By committing ourselves to deep inward reflection, we avoid an automatic "deflective" response to incoming communication signals. When we understand the reason why the image is not in focus, we can then fine-tune the lens to fully capture the picture. I was looking at this autoimmune condition with the wrong filter. My body was trapped in abandonment. I observed others' actions with a rejection lens, so my thoughts, behaviours, and words were coming from a malfunctioning channel. To understand and heal our hurts or frailties, we must face the full mind, body, and soul scan. If we are brave enough to look through the scope, we can discover if our signals are coming from a healthy or wounded space.

It wasn't easy for me to step into that full body scan, but I had reached an impasse where it hurt more being in the dark. The fact is, the truth really does set you free (John 8:32). Truth is all about seeing past the distorted and getting clarity. Sometimes we can be so close to something that it feels absolute but because of our very position to it, it's an illusion—think of a mirage. Challenging ourselves to enter the scan to fully see truth is essential for communication.

Obviously, these scans are not physical but figurative. I imagine stepping into an elevator, but to move and get to the right floor, I need to answer a series of questions that transport me to the proper destination. Without providing directions in the way of answers, I would end up just riding an endless elevator with no control of what floor I landed on. The soul scan must be comprised of asking questions and reconciling the answers. The picture of our life will never come into focus if we don't participate in those two things.

When I began to inquire why certain organs were failing me and why I felt a certain way, I was shocked at the answers. The reason is never at the surface. I needed to dig deeper to make the connections. This illness wasn't a freak misfortune. Over the years I have endured collapsed lungs, chest tubes, life-threatening asthma attacks, three miscarriages, countless surgeries, and near-death experiences. My body was literally rejecting life. To see the full picture, I had to begin the question-and-answer scanning process. *Why is my body rejecting itself and what can I do to work towards emotional and physical acceptance? Has rejection become so familiar to me it is now a form of safety?* I am taking the steps to stretch and grow. To become a great communicator, we must master the art of asking questions and then resolve the issues that arise from the answers. When we do that, we can take steps to detox, defrag, and ultimately learn what is the source of the issue. This stimulates restoration. Rinse and repeat. We all have things to heal. It's a continual process. It's not a one and done kind of thing. To attain Captain Communicator status, we must commit to this practice day in and day out for a lifetime. The soul scan is the main component in the BS detector. You cannot BS your way out. Authenticity holds the key.

People often feel stuck because they deem their problems too complicated to find a way out. Every issue is complex, but the path to freedom doesn't have to be. If we could just begin by asking "why?" we would take a giant step forward in the communication journey. *Why* is a little word that packs a powerful punch. With every piece of information we send or receive, we could pause and ask "why." Have you ever been talking to someone, and their comment just sends you into an immediate reaction mode? They obviously pushed the emotional eject button and you lost all control. Have you ever wondered WHY that comment created such a charge in you? Humans often don't ask why, they just react. Asking why and receiving an answer opens the door to accountability. Our ego doesn't like finding out the why. I hear all the time "that's just how I am." Well, why is that? There is no right or wrong answer, it's just a response to a question. But if we refuse to ever learn the why, we keep repeating and contributing to the thievery.

Speaking from experience, the why always scared me. If I asked why, then I would have to take ownership—and how can I be a victim if I am partially responsible? Have you ever been on the receiving end of someone's trigger vomit? You sit there and think *what the heck did I say?* Instead of pausing and asking ourselves why they were charged, we react right back in turn. It's a vicious cycle and only the soul scan can decode those messages to break the pattern. The soul scan is a filtration system. So, when confrontations and emotions surface, how do the body, mind, and soul affect interpersonal exchange? If we don't consciously create a communication release system, we just continue to absorb. Eventually something will give out. So, the goal is to acknowledge, process, accept, and let go. The full scan is all about the intention of seeing your life from all sides. We cannot know the root cause of issues if we don't have all the information. Though it might be uncomfortable to truly see who we are with no filters, it is necessary in the communication process. Superman doesn't have to be the only one with x-ray vision; we can also attain that superpower. But with that, we also need to face our own nemesis. What is your kryptonite? What lens needs to be cleaned or replaced to achieve crystal clear vision?

Seven years ago, I took a step to reboot my internal communications system. I discovered that I couldn't see anything on the outside clearly or objectively because I wasn't seeing myself clearly. That's the thing about the 360 scans: the inside view transforms the outside one. You see, my dad is still alive. Only in recent years has mental health become safe to speak about. Before then, it was taboo and therefore shameful. No one admitted if they were struggling, especially not men. My dad was going through a challenging time. He camouflaged his pain and decided to leave. History ended up repeating itself. Father conceals his agony. Daughter masks her torment. The disguise became a recurring generational curse.

My dad returned home shortly after leaving. For the longest time I lived in the land of rejection, abandonment, and resentment. I had no x-ray vision because I was completely blinded by the trauma itself. But once I began addressing my own foggy filters, I began to improve my eyesight. The pictures we see play a massive role in the signals we send and receive. I started to look at my father through a new lens. With this new clarity, I discovered mercy and grace. The more I accepted myself and my imperfections, the more I could accept others. What ended up happening was me realizing my dad is the hero in this story. He was the gallant one that paved the way for me to respond to his bravery. He changed the course of his life by following the path home. His acceptance is the healing balm to my body's rejection. Dad, you are forgiven, wanted, and belong. Our connection is safe. Superheroes aren't bulletproof. We all fall and fail, but the ones who get back up and try again are the true protagonists. It was from that place of healing that wires began to reconnect and systems started to work again. After years of living on autopilot, I took over the controls and became the captain of my life.

CHAPTER

2

LIVING MY RELIGION

F-BOMBS

I grew up in a Christian home where my childhood consisted of Sunday school, community gatherings, and faith principles. I learned from an early age the importance of communicating with kindness and embodying a moral code that would reflect our faith values. The golden rule was always something that accompanied my actions and words. I'm not sure if it was naiveness or trusting to a fault, but in my adulthood I expected that anyone who claimed to be Christian would also emulate these standards. This has been a real eye-opener for me. People don't necessarily follow these exact ideals or have the same interpretations. Just because we claim to believe in God doesn't mean we live with God integrity. At thirty-seven years old, I encountered my first Faith Bomb attack.

It all started when I published my first book *Heroine: Embrace Your Flaws & Own Your Awesome.* The cover has a woman posing in her underwear. The theme is all about becoming unmasked and celebrating our imperfections as well as our strengths. This one photo has made me a target of criticism, judgment, and condemnation amongst Christian women. I was appalled at their response. These people knew me. They knew my heart. They have seen my actions mimic our beliefs and yet that one photo was the catalyst to an all-out religious war. They said it was blasphemy, and I was shunned by my own faith community. It took years of deep work to recover from that F-Bomb attack. My internal communications system interpreted those assaults as rejection—a trauma my wounded heart couldn't manage. I call it an F-Bomb because it came at me like an atomic barrage. The perpetrators call it "Christian Correction" and then validate their assaults under the guise of faith.

Reflecting upon my past, I realized that during all the times my family and I struggled, we had never heard a peep from anyone in our faith circle. Yet when I stepped out and attempted to walk in my purpose, *that* ruffled their feathers and caused many to have an opinion on my life choices. Why? We should be more focused on our own personal and spiritual growth instead of judging others. "You hypocrite, first take the plank out of your own eye, and then you will see clearly to remove the speck from your brother's eye" (Matthew 7:5 NIV). I realize now what I'm doing is disrupting the status quo, and most of the time disruption isn't met with welcomeness. I get it, but when we are committed to following a certain religion or faith then aren't we bound to try to uphold and communicate with those very values we've pledged allegiance to? There was a time when WWJD (what would Jesus do) was a fad and a code of conduct to live by in this world. When did we forget that concept? Do people think that only applies to actions and not to words as well? The F-bombs I was experiencing were not Jesus-like. Aren't we taught to embody a Godkind of love and empathy to all humankind with everything we say and do? If so, WWJD should be accompanied by WWJS (what would Jesus say).

I was wounded, violated, and tormented by the backlash and the complete disregard of the golden rule. Christian women literally judged my book by its cover and made every attempt to tell me it was not of God. Sadly, nothing these women declared had anything to do with our faith but more to do with their own beliefs, triggers, jealousies, and traumas. They took their own oppression issues and projected them onto me. The reason I am speaking about my religion and these experiences is because they have played a vital role in teaching me communication strategies. How would I learn how to effectively respond to bullies and pushback if I wasn't challenged? Because I had not yet processed my earlier traumas, I was not good at dealing with conflict. My sympathetic nervous system was always leading the charge in those conversations, and I could never effectively send or receive proper signals. However, when I encountered the F-Bomb attacks, I was given the opportunity to learn how to better receive criticism.

My husband would tell me that there will be people who won't like or understand my book or work and that I am going to have to find a way to manage without taking it as a massive rejection. With his help, I slowly began to examine each attack to figure out a better way to receive people's signals. I can't help it if someone takes issue with what I'm saying or doing, but when they come at me, it is my responsibility to receive and respond with maturity, grace, and wisdom. This is how we stop the identity theft.

Emotions and coping mechanisms should be our sidekicks, but if provoked they may take the leading role and render us a passenger in our own life. So, when our perspective is challenged or when we feel invalidated, I suggest a five-second pause. This pause allows us a moment to self-regulate, collect our thoughts, and receive incoming signals. These five seconds give us time to truly process what is happening in the moment and enable us to adopt an appropriate approach. People are always giving tells; we just have to be in the right space to interpret them.

The silent pause is a trick to successfully receive information, but it also works for the response. It's easy to deliver and read information when it's a good interaction but when we meet opposition, we forget all the tools we have learned. When I received resistance or criticism from the general public, I was able to recognize (in that pause) that my words had charged them because they are dealing with a form of trauma or negative self-esteem. I have taken training on this and done extensive research.[1] I have also done the work on myself and see the progress in my own self-image. I handle these situations like a boss. But when it came to dealing with people in my faith, I needed a lot more work. Part of the reason was that I never in my wildest dreams imagined other Christians would take issue with what I'm doing. Granted, my cover photo is a bit more risqué for traditional religious types, but I thought the spirit of the book would override initial feelings surrounding that picture. How could learning to love myself, helping others heal, and empowering women to breathe fire be un-Christian? Doesn't the Bible corroborate my mission? "So God created man in his own image, in the image of God created he him; male and female created he them" (Genesis 1:27 KJV). I believed a lie my whole life that I was unworthy. I finally realized the truth: I am made in His image. Everyone is beautifully and wonderfully made. Why should other Christians take issue with my newfound freedom?

Through trial and error, I found an effective way to respond to attacks. Rarely will any side convert the other in heated conversations, but it is possible to all walk away with a better understanding of each other. I make a conscious effort to ask questions rather than attempt to satisfy the other with answers they did not want to hear. When I was in that defensive position, I had handed over power to the other side. Now I simply reply to criticism with a question. "What is in my book that a Christian woman shouldn't do?" The answer is nothing. It might not be filled with scripture verses and conventional language, but my book and work are Godly. When I don't want to enter a debate, I respond with, "Thank you for sharing your opinion. I appreciate you feeling comfortable to share with me." Then I exit the conversation, and most often it disarms people. I still get F-Bombed on a regular basis, but now with improved firewalls and strategies, I just get flesh wounds—not heart ones.

EAT PRAY LOVE

Prayer is a key component in the Christian communications system. In a nutshell it is a two-way transmission practice. We glorify and pray to receive guidance, hope, healing, and peace. Our messages are delivered with a certain trust in our God—we give and receive. A distinct prayer I voiced in 2016 changed the trajectory of my life. I was grieving from my first miscarriage and had spiralled into a deep depression. My broken heart and my battling for my life with this autoimmune disease took me to an incredibly bad place. One day as I was sobbing on the couch, I looked at my phone and scrolled through Facebook. I saw a post about a healing minister coming from Texas to Alberta in a few weeks. I didn't know her, but I thought I recognized her name. It turns out there was a connection. Her parents were healing ministers who visited my church when I was little, and they left a lasting impact on me. The "Happy Hunters" (no relation to me) have since passed on and their daughter, Joan Hunter has taken over their ministry. I instantly felt this pull to go see her. I called my mom to take me because I was too ill to drive, and she agreed. As we drove, I prayed, "God, I need a sign tonight that I'm not going to die and there is still some hope for my life. I don't care what it is but if you are really with me, I need my sign." As we entered the building, I led my mother to the front and sat down but my mom hesitated, "Not this close." I simply replied, "I didn't come here for the back." She sat down beside me, and the service began.

When Joan Hunter was speaking, I got loud in my head and uttered the same prayer, "God I need my sign. I will stay in this chair all night if I have to, but I am not leaving here without my sign." Then out of nowhere she declared in the middle of her sentence that someone is drawing on her so much, she can't continue.

Everyone went quiet and still. Then she walked over to me and looked me right in the eye and said, "God hears your cry. He sees your pain. The tears will end. Joy will come and you will write a book about it." This was my sign. I left that service injected with a new-found hope for my life that God isn't finished with me yet.

Prayer doesn't need to be a complicated ritual. I have always had silent conversations in my head and chatted with God like he was a friend sitting beside me. Prayer is really about your intent and your heart. Many theologists, pastors, leaders, and scientists have attested there is a supernatural power that accompanies prayer, like a mental and spiritual vision board. My purpose, my book, and this path were all a result from a powerful prayer that was validated by a respected leader in the Christian space. Why then do so many Christians oppose what I do? Believers have missed the point if they can't see through their own prejudices to allow room for me in our faith. A central part of prayer is communication, and to truly communicate we must allow for differences. These may include styles, accents, dialects, tones, interpretations, views, and feelings. When I share the story of Joan Hunter being a conduit of an answered prayer, guess what happens? Non-Christians tear up and are deeply moved by this encounter, but Christians turn their noses up at me and dismiss it. They are not open to a unique version of what the typical Proverbs 31 woman is "supposed" to look or speak like. What does that say about our faith? I think we have cut the lines of communication and the meaning of prayer and Christianity entirely. We have gone drastically off course regarding the purpose of communicating with God and others. If one prays one way and then speaks another, there is a communication breakdown within.

Prayer is like a bank account; it's all about the deposits and withdrawals. We pray to honour God and show adoration. Then we rely on receiving comfort and peace from the intimate prayer exchange. It only works when the giving and taking are balanced. We can't just be takers; we must also contribute to the account. I pray to enrich my life, but I also advocate for others with my words. Have you ever noticed the phrasing of your prayers? Do you inject your own opinions or wishes for yourself and others, or do you simply ask God to protect and propel the people in your life? It is quite easy to put our own spin on what we think someone's life should look like. I check myself for that all the time. I might not understand or agree with someone's path but it's none of my business and not my call. My only job in praying for others is to join the petition that good things will happen to them. Our thoughts, words, and prayers hold immense weight. Either they heal or they hurt. Don't you ever be the prick.

"Death and life are in the power of the tongue" (Proverbs 18:21 KJV). We should never underestimate the force of our declarations. This also applies to utterances about our own life. How often do we pray for something, and it doesn't happen? I had to change my approach to praying. Prayer is not about me but about how to praise God. "Not my will, but thine, be done" (Luke 22:42 KJV). Appreciate those seven crucial words the next time in prayer. Though God can influence all things for good, his gift is not necessarily what we expect. As Christians, God must be at the forefront. His will done. His way in our lives. Prayer establishes companionship and love. It also is a way to feed our souls. We cannot allow viruses to come in and infect our prayers. Once our hearts and intentions are contaminated, we feed on the wrong things and our communication lines become polluted. Like I mentioned before, my prayers are like talking to a friend. I picture me receiving connection and contributing to the alliance. Prayer is the ultimate love language and grows in strength with numbers. "For where two or three gather in my name, there am I with them" (Matthew 18:20 NIV). Aim to have a power partner who fights for you and prays with you. Yet remember, we are not alone. No matter where you are in your faith life, God has never left you or forsaken you even when people have. Christians have disqualified me, disapproved of me, cursed me, tried to ruin me, and betrayed me—yet God still grants me favour. I don't answer to those people, I answer only to my God.

HYPOCRITICAL OATH

From my interactions with Christians over the years, I have noticed a deadly virus that has infected many churches and believers—hypocrisy. When I first published *Heroine* and experienced all the attacks from Christian women, I wondered why this was happening. It wasn't just a couple of times; it has been weekly for the last four years. Could my book cover, the things I'm talking about, and the very concept of women empowerment be attacking a religious concept? My approach is challenging and unconventional, but the premise of what I do and say is all built on the teachings that God created everyone in his own image, and we should love ourselves. If God is perfect and he created us in his image of that perfection, then aren't we all perfectly imperfect? He didn't get it wrong with me or you. We are a masterpiece. That is the message I speak about. We all have flaws and things to work on, but we are perfection in his eyes and valuable and precious. For most of my life I didn't see myself through the lens of God. Because of a divine appointment with Joan Hunter, I had spiritual eye surgery. Now it is my mission to help other women, Christian or not, to see themselves with better vision as well.

I get confused when Christian women are triggered by a notion that we are amazing just as we are. That we can love and appreciate our bodies while also being a righteous woman. That we have a purpose beyond having a supporting role to men. Don't their reactions contradict the Bible? There are endless scriptures telling Christians to not judge, to love our neighbour as ourselves, to always let humility win over ego, and to be peacemakers not war-starters. So, when I'm attacked for doing what the Bible tells us to do, isn't that hypocritical? They call my book and my work a sin but then they violate five other commandments in the process. There is a definite communication breakdown happening in the faith world. I think some religious types look at me and think I am a wannabe preacher, but I'm not. My journey, career, and crusade were never about my faith per se. I sought after changing the narrative of my story. That's it. Organically, other women responded to my vulnerability, and this grew into a business. I am a writer, consultant, speaker, and humanitarian who happens to be Christian. So when I write something or talk on stage, I am baffled as to why I must quote scripture to validate my beliefs. When's the last time you asked your massage therapist for scripture verses that endorse hot stone treatments? Of course, you wouldn't do that. That's silly. So why is my profession any different?

Did you know there are two books in the Bible that don't mention God at all? Esther and Song of Solomon never reference God, but these are prime examples of the powerful undertone of how God influences lives in subtle ways. Esther's life is a paradigm of how often the behind-the-scenes presence is more powerful than a visible one. It is evident God was working in Esther's life to position her to fulfill her destiny. The story is filled with hope and a supernatural pull. Joseph was another example in the Bible where God didn't seem to be there for him in a visible sense. He spent thirteen years in jail for a crime he didn't commit. But throughout that time, things were falling into place for Joseph to rise as one of the most powerful men in Egypt. It would be highly hypocritical to judge someone based solely on what we see with the naked eye. That is not Christian. I would rather err on the side of caution and say, "Bless Them," rather than curse another with my judgment. We may not know what someone's purpose is. Let us use our words to encourage people to fulfill their destiny instead of tripping them up with our two-faced jabs.

Every day I am persecuted by people who refuse to seek a better understanding. They choose to not make room for me and actively cut the communication lines between us. I am not the enemy. We are on the same team. Maybe we will never fully understand one another but as Christians we are mandated to try. Our faith depends on its people working together and demonstrating unconditional love. I think people can get caught up in defending their principles and thus lose sight of the main goal. We must go back to the greatest commandments given to Christians by Jesus himself: "'Love the Lord your God with all your heart and with all your soul and with all your mind. This is the first and greatest commandment.' And the second is like it: 'Love your neighbor as yourself'" (Matthew 22:37-39 NIV). Whatever our intent is, if our words or actions contradict these two commandments, we are embodying a fraudulent faith. This explains why so many people oppose Christianity—we are walking hypocrites. Society isn't rejecting morals; they are refusing self-righteous egos. Can you imagine a world in which all Christians practiced what they preached? This would instill curiosity. Judgement and ego stop communication, but grace and humility build bridges. Christians need to get back to reflection not deflection. I never wanted to have this conversation but somehow, I accidently uncovered a silent virus festering below the surface of my church—oppression masked with sanctimony.

God isn't looking for religious box checkers; he's looking for people who love the unlovable. So many people are saying the right things, looking the part, and seem like the "ideal" Christian but it's all smoke and mirrors. I used to be a box checker. I showcased the perfect package of what a Christian girl should look like, but I was hiding all the mess inside and regrettably, I hurt others as well.

It was an Oscar-worthy performance but it didn't win me any brownie points with God. I wasn't following the mantle of my faith or my purpose. I had also turned my nose up at others who didn't fit the mould. I had unhealthy communications systems throughout my inner and outer world. I worked so hard on the image I was projecting, but I never strengthened my soul. I was violating the second greatest commandment—love your neighbour as yourself. There are actually three superior commandments named later in that scripture verse. Jesus clearly states that to love others, we must love ourselves first. All my self-image work is therefore part of fulfilling my Christian duty. By halting my acting and allowing the messy to be exposed, I could finally realize God loves me just as I am, flaws and all. The fewer boxes I checked, the closer I got to fulfilling my destiny and embodying love.

This is something we must work towards. We need to do away with the perfected mask and get back to the heart of what our faith is about—love. "If I give all I possess to the poor and give over my body to hardship that I may boast, but do not have love, I gain nothing. Love is patient, love is kind. It does not envy, it does not boast, it is not proud. It does not dishonor others, it is not self-seeking, it is not easily angered, it keeps no record of wrongs. Love does not delight in evil but rejoices with the truth. It always protects, always trusts, always hopes, always perseveres" (I Corinthians 13:3-7 NIV). Every human no matter what religion they believe in needs to return to this concept. Love is a universal language. Love shatters hypocrisy. Love heals humanity. A soft and tender heart is the Christian superpower.

COVID CONTROVERSY

I'm going to touch on a controversial topic, but it is imperative not to shy away from it. The Bible is ALL about teaching us how to both receive God's love and give God's love. This sounds like a spiritual communications system to me. During the pandemic I have seen countless severed connections. Where is the love? I am reminded of the childhood expression, *Ready or not, here I come.* I believe in these times, Christians are playing a spiritual game of hide-and-go-seek. Yet our goal shouldn't be to hide love; we should be seekers of it. Jesus says our second greatest assignment is to love our neighbour as ourselves. But aren't we instead hiding or covering up that directive to love? We have allowed our ego to be the pursuer. Let's now seek out our blind spots. This distorted game of hide-and-go-seek has exposed more hypocrisy. We, as a religion, have muddied the waters with countless dos and don'ts and taken on the attitude of "Do as I say, not as I do." Christians are now seeking an image rather than pursuing love. They are hunting for selfish gain instead of searching to help others. This approach cuts the connection feed with God.

Where is the compassion? Why has COVID-19 become a political tug-of-war instead of a conduit to show the unfailing love of God? Christians have lost sight of the assignment—to be a defender of love. God does not want us to play a part in the tug-of-war at the expense of our relationship with him or at the cost of others knowing him. The pandemic has affected the entire world, so I'm perplexed as to why this has become a religious battle. My religion has hidden love and sought rage instead.

I cannot fathom why some Christians outrightly disobeyed social distancing laws and government policies. The mask mandate wasn't about masking up our religious rights. I am embarrassed by the attacks, bullying, and disrespect shown by people who call themselves Christians. Where was the restraint and trust that God will fight our battles? Instead of approaching disagreements with diplomacy and wisdom, many Christians turned to rabble-rousing means. When citizens or other believers followed the mandates, some Christians accused them of living in fear. Yet even if someone is living in fear, does mocking or criticizing ever work? When I need to change my course, it is not a firm rebuke that motivates me to see the error of my ways and shift my perspective. Instead, it's the encouragement and prayer from others as well as the gripping love of the Holy Spirit that soften my heart. Some Christians have become tyrants.

As I reflect on their inconsiderate tactics and the possible motivation behind them, I see that these bullies are triggered, their religious ideals and belief systems challenged. When we as humans face a threat, our amygdala activates our flight, fight, freeze, or fawn response. If we have not trained our minds, we will fall victim to our flesh and react impulsively rather than respond calmly in faith. Christians clearly need more teaching and discipleship in this area. They tend to think of flesh as sexual immorality, but I think of the term flesh in a bigger sense as it relates to our minds and egos.

We sing about the reckless love of God and how we need to embody this kind of love, yet we are not doing it. We cannot claim to live a Christ-like life and then go take laws into our own hands, torment, make fun of, or hurt others. That is Christian hypocrisy.

I know I need a daily reality check, and I always pose reflective questions to myself. I ask God if I need an attitude change, and most of the time, I do. I don't want to be a hypocrite. I don't want to deter someone from accepting Christ into their heart. I don't want to cause discord or cause pain for my own selfish gain. I want to be an advocate for peace and be a champion for the love of God. I want to seek love and embody the three greatest commandments in the Bible. How can we, as Christians, fight against the mask or vaccinations and not fight for racism to end with the same outrage? How can we protest the closing of our churches when we don't show our love for God with all our hearts, with all our souls, and with all our minds when they are open? We shout at sporting events but remain silent during praise and worship. Why are we not unmasked spiritually in church? I see the social media posts and the anger and frustration. I see the accusations that our rights and our faith are being attacked and violated. Where is the same passion and drive to fight for women's rights and voices? Where is the uprising to end child and sex trafficking? Who is making noise about domestic abuse? Why aren't we protesting homelessness and hunger? Who is going to wave the flag against gun violence? Where are the seekers of love for others? I just see lovers of self.

The pandemic unveiled people's true character. Just as we see new variants of COVID-19 emerge, another destructive variant has surfaced in Christianity—entitlement. What I have witnessed across North America is sickening. Are we so entitled as a culture that we can't even see how good we have it? There are countries around the world begging for medical intervention and the opportunity to be safe, but we in North America call those very things communism or totalitarianism and infringements of our rights. I challenge everyone to go to some of these war-torn or impoverished countries and see what hell the people live in. We need a wake-up call from our first-world privilege. I'm not going to debate whether we should get the vaccine or not. This really isn't about the coronavirus pandemic at all; it's about upholding the values of Christianity. People can be against the vaccine and question the motives of the government, but this isn't about religious persecution. No one is telling us we cannot worship our God. The government isn't killing people for having a certain faith. If churches were the only places shut down and if Christians were the only ones being restricted, then our religion would have an argument. But that wasn't the case. The entire world has had to adjust, accept, and follow these measures. It seems like Christians got their toy taken away and the bulk of the people decided to throw a massive temper tantrum.

Events and behaviours with the freedom convoy in early 2022 are the opposite of Christ-like living. Granted, not everyone there was Christian, but the fact there were flags with scripture verses printed on them and people singing about God is a disgrace. When we stand by a flag that says F*CK the leader/government, we aren't embodying Christian morals. Nothing about what happened with this uprising was in line with WWJD. We are not above the law even if we disagree. Christians cannot cherry pick what rules to follow. "For rebellion is as the sin of witchcraft, and stubbornness is as iniquity and idolatry" (1 Samuel 15:23 KJV). Apostle Paul cautioned us in Romans 13 to obey the laws of the government because God has ordained them for the purpose of harmony. Orderly and lawful practices are good and protect all citizens. Everyone must adhere to the governing authorities because God founded those very establishments. If we do not respect the laws in place, we are showing disdain towards God.

I have heard Christians use one scripture passage as a loophole to this mandate. "We ought to obey God rather than men" (Acts 5:29 KJV). People used this as a call to disobey pandemic laws. They think masks and vaccines contradict the law of God, and therefore we are to disobey the law of the land and obey God's law instead. Nowhere in the Bible does it tell people to not wear masks or get vaccines. In fact, throughout the Bible we are told to put humanity ahead of our own needs: "Do nothing out of selfish ambition or vain conceit. Rather, in humility value others above yourselves, not looking to your own interests but each of you to the interests of the others" (Philippians 2:3-4 NIV).

Even if the law contradicts the Bible and we stand up for our religious freedom, we are to accept the government's authority over us. This includes any consequences from our decisions. This is demonstrated in Acts 5:41 when Peter and John did not protest being flogged, but instead rejoiced that they suffered for obeying God. Christians can say no to the vaccines and the laws of the land, but we are required to pay the price. Who is willing to die, be jailed, or restricted for their values? "Freedom Fighter" is a cool label to take on, but be prepared to risk everything. I'm disappointed in some pastors during this time. Few openly objected to the protests; instead, many took a silent approach. This silence granted a loud permission to their congregation. So why remain silent? I suspect that if church leaders condemned the freedom convoy, they feared people would revolt and leave their church for another that aligned with their views. Since tithing is the financial base of a ministry, we saw minsters choose money over morals.

I know many disagree with me and that's fine. Some mock my view because they think they were peacefully protesting. Yet when we disturb communities with horns and gang mentality and disrupt food transportation, those are forms of terrorism and that isn't peaceful, patriotic, or Christian. Over twenty million dollars were raised for this convoy yet where are the mass donations for other more dire causes? The money was for food, fuel, and hotels but how many people gave to their local shelter? Where is the self-reflection? If we don't ask ourselves, "Am I wrong?" daily, then we are being ego-led instead of heart-led. I could be very wrong with my views, but this conclusion wasn't made lightly or in haste.

During the height of the pandemic, I felt many Christians were out of line in saying their religious rights were being violated. When I realized I hadn't the faintest clue what our human rights were, I set off on a quest to educate myself. Taking a stance on human rights without knowing about them would have been grossly arrogant of me. I became a certified human rights consultant through an amazing organization in Washington, DC. From there I acquired the background knowledge and tools to help me formulate an opinion. I asked questions and sought input from lawyers, researchers, humanitarians, theologists, pastors, and diplomats. After hundreds of hours of research and digging, the facts confirmed my initial suspicions: something about this movement is not right. It's fuelled by rage and rebellion, not diplomacy and peace. This is anything but Christian. I sat quietly observing for two years before openly taking a stance on this issue. I equipped myself with intel and wisdom to write this book and to continue the dialogue going forward. I extend an invitation to have an open and curious conversation with other viewpoints. I hope to find both Christians and non-Christians who can approach these discussions with the same intrigue and open-mindedness.

In 2022, I represented Canada at a human rights summit in Istanbul, Turkey, where over fifty countries gathered to stand up for human rights and peace. So many issues were brought to light, but it was the absence of one that piqued my interest. Not once in a room of 150 people from all over the world did COVID-19 or vaccinations ever get brought up, being so low on the radar of human rights violations. How refreshing and poignant! Representatives were there advocating for others, not themselves.

I am not here to judge or argue but to highlight possible blind spots, call out hypocrisy, bring awareness to the internal persecution, offer a different take, and bridge the gap of our communications. I don't think Christians realize the messages they are sending out. In all honesty I have contemplated leaving the concept of church and Christianity entirely because of what I have faced, from personal attacks to seeing the responses of the pandemic mandates, the Capitol Hill riot, and US politics. I am embarrassed by my religion. It is my profound encounters with my God—not people—that keep me loyal to my faith. I hope my words stir hearts; we are fighting the wrong battle. This isn't about standing up against COVID-19 or each other, but about wrestling against the virus of animosity. Bible teacher Lisa Bevere shares, "It's like the church has an autoimmune disease and we are attacking our own body."[2] A silent and deadly strain has infected the entire world, including Christians. We allowed conflict to grow and then added a dash of discord with a pinch of self-righteousness and a smidgen of apathy. Christians have followed this recipe. Believers are distracted from honouring the greatest mandates. A concocted potion has put the world in a deep slumber so that they don't know their purpose, don't live with passion, don't understand grace, and have misplaced their anger. The game is poisoned. Love is the only antidote for this virus. If we enter a trigger mode because of our survival responses to fear or challenges, then let us go to the Word of God for the remedy. "There is no fear in love; but perfect love casteth out fear" (1 John 4:18 KJV).

The religious trauma I endured has played a major role in my comms systems being so jumbled. Deciphering what is God-centered as opposed to religious indoctrination has been exceptionally trying for me. Church has become a torture chamber instead of a place of refuge. I have anxiety attacks entering a church because I'm so done with the taunting, bullying, and cruelty from Christians. I see people claiming to live a Christ-like life, yet they introduce oppressive laws and impose fear upon others to follow these laws. Meanwhile they protest any regulations imposed upon themselves. And when people don't follow their rules, these so-called Christians deliver a punishing wave of guilt, shame, judgment, and persecution. We haven't evolved or learned to do better. We just repeat archaic and ineffective ideologies that crush the human spirit. The oppressed have become the oppressors. Friends, family, and strangers have emotionally raped me. It's only by the grace of God that I found a way to heal, forgive, and reply with love instead of hostility.

God is searching for people to pursue his love and bring his antidote to the masses. He is calling upon his warriors to enter the battle and advance the kingdom by spreading the power of his love. This is how we demolish the walls of hatred. His precious love has always been in the open. We just need to unmask it. That is what my faith is all about. So, when I am in the presence of other Christians, I don't cower. I don't get distracted by the tyrants. I say to God, "It's just you and me." When we can free ourselves from the real religious persecution, we unearth the mightiest superpower—love. Today I denounce the hypocritical oath and accept the pledge of sincerity and humility. Our commitment to humility will dissolve the hypocrisy. Living my faith has been the greatest training to relinquish the hold rejection and abandonment had over me.

CHAPTER
3

COUPLE
CONVERSATIONS

MESSAGES SENT

What is the biggest challenge when it comes to relationships? Time and time again people respond, "communication issues." Every single person transmits messages differently. Because we each have our own language frequency, we experience friction and crossed signals when we don't know how to properly decode incoming messages. Our genetics, upbringing, and life experiences shape how we send and receive information. Although much of the world couples up, few of us know how to communicate as a pair. Many try to address the issue by going to therapy, attending counselling sessions, or by reading endless blogs and books. But what if people worked on themselves first before entering any kind of relationship? If we don't know ourselves, heal our traumas, and understand why we communicate the way we do, any relationship we pursue will be susceptible to crossed wires. How can we effectively transmit messages if our own internal communications system is malfunctioning? To ensure a healthy partnership, we must heal the individual beforehand. When I first met my husband, I was living in a world of trauma, and I didn't communicate well at all. It wasn't until we were married for seven years that I mended myself. The only reason we are still married is because I found a way to reconnect all the fragmented pieces and regain proper signals again. I wish I had done that before I met him. It would've saved a lot of heartache, but I can't be faulted for what I didn't know. I'm just so grateful I fixed the systems when I did. Now, I truly know myself and can communicate with love and respect instead of resorting to reactive rebuttals.

Anyone with a smartphone has a love/hate relationship with autocorrect. Sometimes it's your friend and other times it's your foe. Either way, we always have an opportunity to correct a sent message in our digital correspondence. "Oops, sorry, autocorrect…" usually follows my messages. I wish it was that easy with verbal communication. Why do we have a double standard when it comes to speaking with our loved ones? You hardly ever hear people say something mean and then immediately correct themselves and rephrase it. With smartphone autocorrect we tend to shrug it off and laugh. There are tons of memes about it and whenever I need a good chuckle, I read those hilarious autocorrect fails on social media. But when we say something to our partner that is wrong or is misinterpreted, unfortunately we don't have a built-in autocorrect feature. We must manually do it. This takes immense humility and self-discipline. It's like the toothpaste analogy: once it's out of the tube, it can't be put back. It's much better to be conscious of what we are about to say and how it might be received rather than to rely on an after-the-fact corrector. We have the power to control our communications. We can decide how we want our signals to be communicated and translated. It takes work but it is worth the effort. Can you imagine how your conversations will go with this kind of intent? I have focused a lot of attention on how my words are transmitted and on how my husband receives them. Sometimes there is nothing wrong with the actual words, but if he is tuned in to a different signal, then we are speaking two different languages and the result is a communication breakdown. Messages have a better chance of being received well if we each become a committed communicator.

Throughout this book, you will see me refer to many points using "men" and "women" language. I write from the perspective of what I know as a white, heterosexual, cisgender woman. I want everyone to feel included in this dialogue and extend an invitation for learning, understanding, and empathy. Gender is complex and unique to each of us. Involving more than just men versus women, I affirm people of all genders—cisgender, transgender, non-binary, gender fluid, agender, and any other genuinely held gender identity. I am not "gender neutral" or "gender blind;" instead, I seek to acknowledge every person's journey as they explore their own identity. I am working towards a world that recognizes and celebrates every community member's uniqueness.

Do you know what type of communicator you are? I find a lot of people know how their partner communicates but rarely reflect on what their own transmission style is. Everyone might have their own distinguishing communication fingerprint but according to motivational speaker Tony Robbins, we all tend to fall into one of four categories: passive, aggressive, passive-aggressive, and assertive. Passive communicators keep their emotions inside and are the ones who can never seem to say "no." Aggressive communicators are loud and intense, but typically have trouble making real connections with others. Passive-aggressive communicators avoid conflict and use sarcasm to deflect real communication. The healthiest type of communicator is the assertive one: these people are in touch with their emotions and know how to communicate them effectively.[1]

If you don't know which you are, I suggest asking your partner when you are in a calm space. Invite a truthful evaluation mixed with kindness and sensitivity. This is the time to listen and receive helpful feedback on how you are coming across. I know the urge will arise to defend how you communicate, but I encourage you to just allow their information to sink in. This is a crucial step in knowing yourself. We all might have good intentions when we correspond with others, but ultimately their perception of our cues becomes their reality. This might be a hard pill to swallow but it is necessary in creating healthy communication lines. It all boils down to what kind of atmosphere you are committed to having. Words either connect us or separate us. Your commitment to this process is the foundation.

Once you know how you communicate, you can begin to learn, grow, and evolve. Even if you are in the assertive category, you can find areas to improve upon. I had begun healing my trauma and, seeing myself in that assertive group, I thought I was doing well in my communication with my husband—until I asked him. Having read *The Queen's Code* by relationship expert Alison Armstrong, I was prompted to have one of these constructive criticism conversations. I explained the premise of the book to my husband, and we began a discussion about how, in an effort to regain power, some women are emasculating men as their method. Identifying this negative feminine habit was eye-opening for me. I had witnessed other women doing this, but I was sure I wasn't guilty of it. Then in a moment of honesty I asked my spouse, "When I say, 'We are stuck in this town because of you and your job,' does that emasculate you?" He replied, "Yes." My heart pinged. I never wanted to hurt him or make him feel emasculated. I was just frustrated. I also was a bit jealous of him. He had a career he loved, and I didn't at the time. Because my own job was unfulfilling, I had taken a shot at his in a misguided attempt to regain power in the relationship.

From that moment on, I began to shift my words. Don't get me wrong, I still mess up and throw the odd dig in, but I activate the autocorrect when that happens. I have made it my mission to stop trying to de-power the man I love. There's enough authority to go around but it's up to me to step into my personal power rather than steal it from my partner. This kind of intention creates safety within the communication lines. When each person feels safe, the signals flow clearly.

MESSAGES RECEIVED

When we look at communication, we need to steer away from power concepts and move towards empowerment ones. Wouldn't it be amazing if both parties finished a discussion feeling empowered? How often do you leave a conversation, dismayed at the outcome? Perhaps you shared good news but were met with despondency, or you needed encouragement but felt deflated instead. Maybe you required some love and softness, but you encountered a backlash of hostility. Every time this happened, I walked away dumfounded as to how the result wasn't what I had expected. I eventually learned that if I had needs to be met from a conversation, I should be clear at the outset with my hopes and expectations.

People cannot read our minds and as mentioned before, everyone has their own signal frequency. To avoid a translation misfire, we must set up the exchange. Often women need to vent to their partners, but men generally are the fixers. We let our emotions spill and our partners instantly plunge into fix-it mode. They offer suggestions on how to solve the problem, which leads to us getting more infuriated. Have you ever experienced this? The man is confused as to why his partner doesn't want a solution, and the woman is aggravated that her partner isn't listening to her. This is because there was no set up, no preparation or understanding of expectations. The teachings of Alison Armstrong gave me fabulous communication tools. I now go to my husband and say, "Hey, I am having a difficult day and just need to vent, can you hold the bucket for me? I don't need you to do anything or fix it, I just need someone to listen to me and validate that it's ok to feel frustrated." This gave my partner a clear understanding of my needs, and he was able to listen and do what I had articulated. I felt better and he felt helpful because I provided instructions for him to assist me. He knew his job in that moment was to hold space. We both walk away feeling connected, fulfilled, and empowered.

Becoming an empowered communicator is all about being an impeccable translator. Deciphering what lenses and filters your partner's messages are being sent through and knowing which ones you are receiving from are at the helm of this operation. Filters and lenses are basically our personal narratives, the stories we tell about ourselves and others. Many of these narratives are a product of life experiences— the way we grew up, our traumas, the decisions we've made, and the trajectories our lives have taken. Others result from the screen through which we see ourselves, the world, and others. The personal narrative is a matrix. We are the creators of our own reality. We control what image we want. We must also acknowledge the raw information from our partners who have had experiences that shaped their own language. The key to this entire process is to become a referee of your own thoughts and then to put on the detective hat in each conversation. I picture a loud whistle blowing that prods me to halt the "best-seller fiction writing." I pause the scene and then navigate through a series of questions and steps to take control of the narrative.

I take some deep breaths and count to five, then ask myself:

- Do I have all the facts, or do I need more information?
- Is this narrative healthy or harmful?
- Is this true or is my matrix playing tricks on me?
- Is this a "them" issue or am I being triggered here? (It may be one or the other, or both.)
- How can I de-escalate this situation rather than fuel it?
- Am I contributing to this issue? If so, take ownership and apologize.

I then take more deep breaths and remind myself that:

- "I'm ok," "I am safe," and "I don't need to deflect by projecting anger."
- I no longer buy into fictitious scenarios.
- Our brains often don't like "I don't know" as an answer, but we can usually uncover the truth in a moment of calm.
- It's better to extend the pause rather than write fictitious narratives.
- Using language like "when you say that I feel . . ." or "I am being triggered right now; I will get back to you" is safe.
- "I am the writer of this story," and "I choose a healthy plot."

These steps ensure you can transcribe any message received and communicate with wisdom and intelligence.

How we receive messages is directly related to how safe we feel in that space. Remember the mantra "Know Thyself" and take steps to achieve safety within the communication bubble. When we think of being threatened, situations in which we are physically or verbally attacked top the list. But there's also the matrix I mentioned before, where certain word choices, settings, types of people, and personalities have the potential to create a sense of danger within, even if the words themselves are non-threatening. These expressions or scenarios may push the trigger button and activate our fight, flight, freeze, or fawn response. Remember, we each have a past that has fashioned us into the people we are, and this includes how we receive information. We are all from diverse planets, many more than the simple saying "Men are from Mars, women are from Venus." We all have triggers. This means we must commit to knowing what prompts our reactive response so we can verbalize the trigger and create safety within our relationships.

Since I have had some bad experiences with men in the past, when I communicate with any person who has a more of an aggressive or masculine personality, I tend to be meek and cautious. My trigger alarms are set off, warning me: "Danger Alert." I now recognize that when I'm in that space, I don't feel safe and consequently receive mixed messages with completely wrong signals. Most of the time these people are not attacking me but since I feel unsafe, I become endangered. Knowing all this was so helpful for me to achieve a better connection with my husband.

Now, I set him up for success in communication with me by telling him, "When you say [...], I feel like a bad wife or bad mom, and this makes me feel inadequate and therefore not safe to talk to you." He listens to me verbalize a feeling and now he doesn't use certain words or phrases. We avoid a lot of the landmines and triggers because I figured out what was contributing to my peril. Honesty with humility builds a safe place in a relationship. Safety builds trust within the partnership, and trust strengthens the lines of communication. Trust disarms the triggers.

What stories are we telling ourselves each day? Are they Fact or Fiction? Do they Help or Hurt us? Our internal and external communications are written by our own mental pen. We compose a storyline from the scenes we encounter. Our physical lives then respond to what is birthed in our minds. We can't change events from the past, but we do have the influence to alter the course of our present and future selves. So, when we are collecting messages and data, we need to trust that they are true stories and not fiction.

Texting is always a difficult way to communicate anything deep because the tone can be misconstrued. Consequently, we must carefully examine any stories we may make up about the person we are speaking with. A prime example is when my husband texted me asking, "What did you spend 200 dollars on at the store?" Because that felt a bit accusatory (and I took it as *I'm in trouble for spending that much*), I immediately when into trigger mode. I made up the narrative that he was upset and I'm going to have to explain why I spent this money. Previously, I would send a long apologetic message explaining why I needed to make the purchase, and add how I am making or saving money elsewhere. This would usually end up in us having a disagreement or me feeling like I did something wrong until I realized he was just literally asking me what I bought. We shifted how we communicate in texts by agreeing to ask for clarification before believing a made-up storyline. Now, when he asks me a question or says something in a text or in person that triggers me, I respond with a question. "Your comment feels a bit accusatory, and I am wanting to go on the defense. Was that the intent of your comment?" This gives him a chance to clarify and stop a disagreement before it starts. Changing the storyline is all about diffusing the triggers, swapping out the filters, shaping the bigger picture, and designing your identity within your relationship. Re-remembering the past is about discovering grace and forgiveness, altering your view of reality, and altering your view of yourself. Always seek clarification. A fuzzy picture results in drama. We are the keepers of our story. We are the masters of the messages we send and receive.

WAR ZONE

When we communicate with our partner, we need to remember to keep the focus on conversation, not combat. They are not the enemy. We are on the same team. Once this concept moves from head knowledge to heart wisdom, we establish connection. If there is conflict, there is a problem that needs solving. Shifting our energy from fighting each other to tackling the crisis together creates a unified front. I know it's easier said than done. When you have different communications styles and various filters and personalities at play, it can be challenging to not engage in a fight. We can, however, disagree respectfully without adding fuel to the fire. This takes self-control and maturity. It's so easy to spark a war of words filled with digs and cheap shots, but that isn't effective communication and it distracts us from the real conflict. I was guilty of this with all my relationships. I got triggered or upset about something and without any effort, low blows poured from my mouth. Throughout my personal growth journey, I came to realize how this stunted my relationships. After hours of intensive arguing, we ended up back where we began, with the exact same problem. We said mean things and fed that fire without putting any energy into solving the real matter. Even if we don't mean to hurt the other person, when we don't realize how they might perceive our words, we will do just that. Communication is not so much about our intentions, but more about how the information is received. The war zone should be about conflict resolution, not word-bombing our significant others.

I like to compare working through conflict to an atom. Every atom is neutral when it contains an equal number of protons and electrons. It is Switzerland. When we have a disagreement or face any kind of conflict, we must remember to be like the neutral atom. We have the right to be upset, but to work through it we must anchor ourselves to the commitment of being uncharged. I hear a lot of people say, "Why should I do this, when my partner doesn't?" I can see how that looks unfair. But do we want to be right and fuel the fight, or do we want to resolve our conflict and be at peace with our partners? It takes one person to be the atom in the combat. Otherwise, we will continue charging the issue. I promise once you embody this neutral-charge mentality, you will see your partner respond in a positive way. When I stopped being the conduit for the charge, the disagreements ended more quickly. There was no fire. I learned how to express my anger and frustration without shaming or blaming my husband— and he started doing the same. Our fights went from hours of fueling the fire to minutes of a controlled burn that quickly extinguished. I challenge myself in a moment of conflict to use wise words and to be the atom. This was a game changer for me. I learned how to be a responsive communicator and not a reactor. Being a neutralizer doesn't mean we should avoid a fight. That is passive and won't assist in the resolve. Atoms are active. They are stabilizers. They are the unsung heroes in the war zone.

When I observe relationships, they tend to fall into two categories: the conflict engagers and the conflict avoiders. In a world with almost eight billion people, why don't we learn more about how to have a dispute? This should be taught in schools, in homes, in churches, and in the workplace. We are going to have many disagreements in our lifetime. But if we don't learn how to navigate through them, we will just resort to faulty coping mechanisms, trauma responses, and unhealthy communication styles. There's a reason so many marriages end in divorce. We simply don't know how to conquer conflict.

As I mentioned before, if we don't do the work on ourselves before entering a relationship, we will face challenges within the partnership. If we have a lack of identity, trust issues, unresolved traumas, or poor communication skills, our relationships will suffer. Those unresolved toxic contributors break down communication in all areas of our lives. Every person in this world needs to collect conflict resolution tools and learn to access that toolbox when in challenging situations. Learning about myself and how men operate allowed for me to understand both what my needs are in the relationship as well as my husband's. In my research, I found that when men don't feel respected in the relationship, they tend to withhold their love. And when women feel unloved, they respond by disrespecting their partner. This toxic pattern continues to repeat over and over without either side realizing what's happening. Unless one of the parties becomes the atom and removes themselves from this merry-go-round, the cycle continues. When we learn how to neutralize, de-escalate, verbalize needs, and listen to our partners in a disagreement, we become the solution.

Becoming the resolver in the conflict doesn't mean you cave, it means you are making conscious choices on how to have a truce instead of an ongoing fight. A peace treaty is a daily commitment for both people in the relationship. Sometimes it's more about acceptance than anything else. I have had to accept that my husband has faults; I cannot change that. I accept that I too have faults; no matter how hard I try and how much it might annoy my partner, those faults will always be there. I recognize we both have filters we send and receive information from, and those filters will cause miscommunication at times. In those moments, being the atom is imperative.

What about with difficult topics like money, sex, kids, parents, desires, dreams, and careers? No matter the subject, the strategy is the same. We will always be two unique people with two different dialects, but learning to decode the filters with love and respect will help bridge the gap in our languages. When we can articulate our needs and wants without shaming or blaming our partners, we automatically remove most of the filters and unhealthy response mechanisms. Applying questions instead of accusations helps to resolve the conflict. It is at this juncture we learn how to decode each other's messages and speak their language.

The argument is no longer a power struggle dance. You both want to put the effort into the resolution rather than the fight. This is where the friction transforms into fusion.

THE APOLOGY EFFECT

Even with the best of intentions to "be the atom" in conflict, we still occasionally let our emotions get the better of us and we revert to old patterns that fuel the fire rather than extinguish it. We need to recognize when this happens, and apologize and forgive one another. Vulnerability and grace are the markers of a healthy and safe relationship. The apology effect is about being the keeper of the trust factor in relationships. If no one takes accountability (or if it's always lopsided), feelings are hurt, trust is broken, and communication lines jam up. Taking ownership for our behaviours, words, and actions is vital for any relationship to succeed. Have you ever found it difficult to apologize? Why is something that should come so naturally to us such a challenge? It's like we must defy all logic and force ourselves to say, "I'm sorry, I was wrong." Verbalizing remorse takes courage.

Is our ego that influential? Is it because we really aren't taught how to apologize? Recently, my family has been modeling taking ownership for our actions and verbalizing apologies. We're better at apologies now, but we had to work at it. I don't think my grandparents apologized to my parents very often, and I don't remember hearing "I'm sorry" much growing up. We were taught to say sorry as kids when we took someone's toy for instance, but after those younger years, it wasn't enforced in schools or reaffirmed in adulthood. Then when we enter the workforce and relationships, we end up with atrophied apologizing skills. Saying sorry should be second nature. We need to get back to the intersect where empathy and the desire to re-connect overrides the need to be right.

Over the last few years, I have been researching and observing various insights on the art of the apology. Some points reaffirmed what I already thought, and others challenged me to the core. I was most impacted by the episode "I'm Sorry: How to Apologize and Why It Matters" of Brené Brown's podcast *Unlocking Us*.[2] It was a two-part series with psychologist, therapist, and apology expert Dr. Harriet Lerner. There's much to unpack, but we will begin with the purpose of an apology. Lerner reveals the apology is a reflection of the amount of self-worth and self-respect a person possesses. I had never looked at it that way. When I am faced with having to take ownership of something I did, it feels like my self-esteem takes a hit. But if we can be brave and apologize, we are demonstrating incredible self-discipline and regard for ourselves. When we can choose the relationship over being the winner in conflict, we become a true champion.

Lerner also explains there's three gifts to an apology. The first is a gift to the person we hurt. It releases them from the anger and resentment of the situation. It allows them to feel safe again, and they get to see their feelings affect us. We show we care about the other's emotional safety and by so doing we validate their reality. The second one is a gift to self. To admit we aren't perfect is a great gift to ourselves and unchains us from the fear of losing control. Apologizing is one of life's treasures that offers us an opportunity to take responsibility and accountability. That is the very basis of self-respect. We might feel small, but we are incredibly tall when we admit our wrongs. We grow in maturity and integrity when we offer heart-felt apologies. The third is a gift to the relationship. We must provide a sincere apology to reinforce trust within the relationship. The cost of not apologizing results in a broken one. It's about repairing the damage.

Even after fourteen years of marriage, I still find it difficult to apologize sometimes. I am, however, committed to an atmosphere of accountability and cohesiveness in my partnership. I regularly practice using language that shows sincerity in my apologies. My husband has taught me a lot in this department. I admire him in that he has no issue admitting fault. We disagree, I provide my perspective, and then he says, "You're right, I apologize." He always had more confidence than me, so maybe that is part of it. To him, taking ownership doesn't make him feel small. I appreciate that in him.

One time, I was extremely upset over something he had said, and instead of overreacting and unloading on him, I simply voiced how those words made me feel unsafe. We made up, but when we went to bed that night, he held me and told me he hears me. I broke down and sobbed. That is exactly what I needed: to be heard. He validated my feelings, and it released me.

According to Lerner, many commit a faux pas when attempting to give or receive an apology. Do we immediately address the offence, or do we stew over it and thus fuel our anger and resentment? We may send a nasty message or email, unleash our grievances face to face, or just avoid that person altogether. But do they even know why we are upset? I am guilty of this. I can feed fictional stories in my head all day about how insensitive my husband is until it turns into an all-out blow up when he gets home. If I had but told him earlier in the day and allowed him the opportunity to diffuse the situation, we both would have been spared grief. We need to have the courage to let the person know we are upset.

The first steps in conflict resolution are to express that there's a problem and begin a dialogue. Start by saying, "When you did that or said this, it made me feel . . ." Then, actively listen. Provide space for the recipient to respond with ownership and a heart-felt apology. Both parties should have an opportunity to listen and be curious about the issue. Both sides must work at this, not just the one in the wrong. It's a dance. Lerner stresses to not be vague when pointing out offenses and to give specific examples. We must not take one or two infractions and declare, "You always do this" or ask, "What kind of person would do that?" Creating a safe place for both people in the relationship is key. This is the time for a meaningful conversation, not an attack of blame and shame. A successful resolution does not even depend on both agreeing on all the facts. It's okay to say, "I see things a bit differently." Express empathy and say, "Thank you for bringing this up to me, I will continue to think about the impact this had on you." In the end if your partner expresses a hurt or an offense, a heart-felt apology is necessary to move forward. Practice the art of the apology. Get comfortable with saying "I'm sorry I hurt you. Your feelings matter to me. I hear you. It is not my intention to cause you pain. That comment or my actions were out of line. I won't do that again."

We often lump apologies with forgiveness, and we need to separate the two. The apology is the birthplace of forgiveness, but we must remember it will take time and other steps in between. Lerner emphasizes a true sincere apology doesn't include the word *but*. It doesn't bring up past grievances; the focus should be on the current problem. Don't over apologize and become the martyr. This isn't about you, but how to listen to someone voice their hurt. A vital thing to remember is to try to be in a calm state of mind. Breathe lots and navigate out of the red zone. We cannot listen when our nervous system is overheated.

Lerner stresses it's better to delay an apology than give a bad one. There are many bad apologies, and they cause more harm to the relationship. Don't say sorry only to justify your actions. This nullifies the apology. A good apology offers a resolution to the situation. It re-establishes cohesiveness. It's not about absolving us of our guilt or making us feel better. An apology is not for you; it is for your partner. We need to apologize even when we think we did nothing wrong. This goes back to deciding the atmosphere to which you are committing. Say sorry for the part you played and don't get caught up in the blame game or in figuring who is more at fault. Lerner shares when someone is being their worst jerk, we are called upon to be our best self. We need to demonstrate self-respect. We cannot wait for the other party to say sorry first. Choose a partnership over division. Challenge yourself to offer a heart-felt apology that presents restitution. Make it right. Demonstrate you heard your partner. Show them with your actions a changed behaviour, not just with your words. Avoid a repeat offense.

In Part 2 of the podcast between Brown and Lerner, they emphasize not getting defensive.[3] Looking for details that are inaccurate and pointing out things we don't agree with are tells of defensiveness, expresses Lerner. However, recognizing that we are triggered and falling into the defensive trap automatically creates some distance from this snare. If we stay in the defensive air space, it will kill the connection. No apology has meaning if we don't understand the other person's pain or anger. Be brave with your accountability and your apology, and demonstrate courage when receiving one. Accept the apology and say thank you, I really appreciate it. Leave it there. Lerner also encourages us to work on bigger issues later, not during the apology itself.

Apologies are not about getting something; they are about giving something. We must therefore receive and release. This isn't about forgiveness; it's about accepting the apology and disarming the negative energy surrounding the issue. Apologies truly are a gift for the relationship. This dialogue between Brown and Lerner is the roadmap of a proper apology and will transform all my communications going forward.

In the podcast series, these women focused on the apology, not forgiveness. They did an excellent job separating the two and showing us how to do the apology right. Now let's focus on the forgiveness part. If we want to move forward in any relationship, we must take ownership of our actions, express remorse, apologize, accept our frailties, apply grace, and work towards forgiveness. This doesn't absolve the wrongdoing but pardons us from holding onto the grievance. Otherwise, this grievance can fester and can cause a complete disconnect from your partner over time. Forgiveness is a sticky wicket. Like most people, I forgive more easily when the person validates my feelings, apologizes, and changes their ways. I struggle when the person, instead of taking ownership of a misdoing and offering a heart-felt apology, would rather allow the relationship to end. I will discuss this more in upcoming chapters, but when strictly talking about our significant others, we must forgive if we want the relationship to have a chance at being healthy and whole.

What does forgiveness look like for you in your relationship? I don't believe "forgive and forget" is practical. Some transgressions are smaller than others and for the heart wounds, we may never fully forget the sting. It's not about forgetting, but accepting. It takes the most courage to forgive. The following is a perfectly poignant and relevant saying attributed to many people: "Keeping resentments is like 'swallowing poison and expecting the other person to die.' The goal is not to forgive and forget, but to grieve and let go."[4] We think if we withhold our forgiveness, we are punishing the other or teaching them a lesson, but we aren't. We only harm ourselves. This fractures the future of a healthy partnership. I'm not saying to just forgive and stay in a toxic relationship. If someone continues to hurt their partner, they are not demonstrating love or respect. In those instances, both parties need to work towards positive change, or break free from the toxicity.

If we don't release the anger, resentment, and bitterness, we invite another being to join our partnership—poison ivy. Every time we choose to not inject grace and actively forgive, we strangle our union with venom. Communication lines are severed. At this point, we as individuals decide the fate of our relationship. So many couples arrive at an impasse when one won't take accountability or the other refuses to forgive. I'm not here to say if your partner cheats on you, to just forgive and move on. Those offences require counselling, serious personal work for both parties, and healing time. But even with infidelity, if we want to stay in the relationship and the other person doesn't repeat the transgression, we eventually must encounter grace and forgiveness. Grace is empowerment. Forgiveness is the ultimate act of self-love and self-respect. Even in situations where it takes me longer to fully forgive my husband and him to fully forgive me, somewhere in the matrix, we reconnect when we both pursue grace. We fight for our relationship instead of against each other. Grace is the secret sauce, the greatest security system within a couple's communications system.

CHAPTER

4

MINI-ME

BE THEIR HERO

"Mirror, Mirror on the wall, who reflects us most of all?" Children often mirror their environment. It's a harsh, but a sobering reality. Are we the heroes or the villains in their story? We grow up with ideals that we will be better parents than the previous generation. But if we don't work on personal growth, how can we expect our children to be any different than what we project? *Do as I say, not as I do* is the social norm, but human behaviour doesn't work like that. Yes, our children are gifted with magnificent qualities from two people, but they also acquire our flaws times two. We need to be mentors of the messages. Our kids are our sidekicks.

What does your home environment reflect? Is it safe? We all have communication breakdowns within our households, and improving the comms within the home is of the utmost importance. Let's start facing the things we need to improve upon. What atmosphere are we committing to with our children? They are the greatest impressionists of all time. My daughter might react and say something, and my husband inevitably responds with, "She's you!" It's quite shocking to witness my own behavior as seen through my child's eyes. Whether it's the good part of me or the not so good, I can't ignore the mirror. We tend to do that; just ignore what we don't like. We need to be aware of how we are sending and receiving messages with our young. To be their hero we don't need to be perfect. Kids aren't looking for perfection, they are craving realness. They require us to commit to safe and authentic communications systems as a whole—myself to me, parent to parent, parent to child.

Various factors contribute to a child's behaviour, but we do have to take responsibility for being their main influence. What kind of communicator do *you* want your kids to be? For children to have the skills necessary to navigate through life successfully, they must witness those skills in action. Ideally, we discover our identity, purpose, and maturity prior to having children, but that usually isn't the case. My daughter was three before I faced the mirror and the music. By age five, she was already mimicking some of my communication styles and fears. I wanted her to be better than me, but I knew that could only happen if I became better. So, over the last seven years, I have dedicated my life to being a Captain Communicator. I choose to face the mirror and demonstrate heroic communications daily. I see her modeling this new way and it's inspiring. Every child comes into this world as a blank canvas and a sponge. They pick up on everything. They are Mighty Receivers and store all that information for the rest of their lives. Let us take a good look at how we are conducting ourselves and be the change we desire. Let us do it for us and for them. Let us lead by example and be vulnerable: acknowledge when we mess up, without deflecting or projecting. Our children need to learn how to recover from a fall and manage a flaw. They cannot succeed without the behind-the-scenes footage. Our future demands that we unmask our past. If we don't learn from our previous ways and shift how we communicate, then our children are doomed to repeat our trials.

Communication is imperative for building strong family relationships, but before we can communicate effectively, we must recognize and value how each person processes information. Whether they are internal or external processors, our kids are decoding and absorbing the entire home's messages at a rapid rate. When we are happy and excited, our children feed off that energy. The same goes for being sad, anxious, angry, or upset. Children want to protect their parents, so they take on their emotions and attempt to process them. The problem with this is that they haven't acquired the proper skills to navigate through adult emotions yet, so we witness an overspill. It may look like acting out or complete temper tantrums, but many times they are just trying to process our crap. They have their own experiences and emotions too, so it is crucial for parents to decipher whose crap is whose.

A perfect example that speaks to this is when we were potty training our daughter. We were doing great with the stickers and the potty chart but then I experienced my first of three miscarriages. I couldn't believe how much my trauma impacted my little one's potty-training progress.

She was a toddler, clueless to what I was going through, yet she could sense the emotional undercurrent of her mama. She completely regressed and wouldn't even poop. We tried every trick in the book to no avail. I grasped that my grief altered the atmosphere in the home, but we all still need to poop, right? I was going to therapy to deal with the loss of my baby, and I had mentioned to the practitioner that my daughter had relapsed in potty training. She wasn't surprised and stated that kids will try to take on their mother's pain and can sense that mom doesn't want to let go of that pain yet. Our pain is their pain. But my mentor reassured me if I get down on her level and explain this wasn't hers to hold, I will see a shift. My heart panged. It's my job to protect her, not the other way around. I went home and sat my precious girl down on the little potty and I crouched on the edge of the tub. Then I looked right into her eyes and explained, "Mommy is dealing with her crap. You don't need to hold onto it for me. Now it's time for you to let go of your crap." No word of lie, she pooped within minutes. This was clearly my crap issue not hers.

Setting the intention of exploring communication as a family unit will unlock mighty superpowers within your home. We won't ever be perfect, but with commitment comes clarity. When we have a clear understanding of how we communicate and how our children need to process information, our comms practices come into focus. Awareness is key. Parents must take ownership and be self-aware to understand the communication needs of the family. Sit down with your partner and children and ask what everyone needs to feel safe to communicate. Ask for every person to try to identify what kind of communicator they are.

External processors like to contemplate out loud. They receive clarity from feedback. Solitude doesn't bode well for them. Overwhelm and anxiety take over when an external processor is left alone during extreme emotions and unanswered questions. Verbalizing to a safe sounding board helps them process their thoughts, fears, needs, and options. An internal processor operates differently. When they encounter intense emotions and queries, they require time alone to carefully contemplate the situation and their decisions. They need to analyze in solitude and chew on possible solutions. When we can appreciate how everyone is hard-wired, we can create space and flow for each person. Through this, families will come to recognize when members are shutting down, and can offer support in the processing stage to those who need it. This will instill safe and productive communication lines.

POSITIVE MENTAL HEALTH = CONNECTED COMMS

Mental, emotional, and physical wellness make up the pulse of a healthy communication system. If we don't have efficient health in those areas, we experience disconnects. We will never be running at 100 percent, but by setting intention on healthy not perfect, we will take strides in bridging those gaps. Mental health in our children is a huge concern these days. We are seeing suicides in kids as young as ten years old, and depression has become an epidemic. How can we combat this? We have so many mental health campaigns, yet they don't seem to be working. The problem is getting worse. Bullying is at the forefront of the issue. If we eliminated internal and external bullying, I am confident we would see depression decline. I absolutely hate Pink Shirt Day, the annual anti-bullying day in February. While I completely support the mission of anti-bullying and acknowledge that Pink Shirt Day has brought awareness to and opened a dialogue surrounding bullying, something is amiss. If all you do is put a pink shirt on your child today and they still bully tomorrow, what is the point? We must change our behaviours, not just our shirts.

When David Shepherd and Travis Price took a stand against bullying in 2007, they initiated conversation. They awakened a kindness culture. Unfortunately, many businesses and schools have bought into this concept only for a day and not a lifetime. Don't wear pink today if you aren't prepared to take a stance the other 364 days of the year. Don't show up to work with a pink shirt today and exclude someone tomorrow. Bullying isn't just mean words or violence; it can also take on a more subtle form. My daughter is excluded at her school, and I continually get left out. Exclusion isn't a form of bullying—it is bullying. Let us tackle the problem at its root and teach parents and children to be reflective and realize that bullying behaviours come from inner hurts. Let's encourage bravery to face those hurts and heal them.

If we don't pick up the mantle of courage in the present moment, aren't we destined to perpetuate the callous culture? The child bully today becomes the tormenting co-worker tomorrow. To reconnect, we must reflect. Choose to look in the mirror. Acknowledge that our critical or judgmental thoughts of others are actually our own feelings of inadequateness. I recognize that my excluding someone is my rejecting myself. This type of intention initiates mental and emotional clarity and ignites connection and healing. As I mentioned before, our children mirror us. So, if they are bullying or being bullied, what does that say about the parents? Are we modeling aggressive communication methods or are we continually showing we are doormats? We must learn conflict resolution strategies and then implement them in our homes so our kids may acquire tools to deal with clashes. We will never be rid of conflict, and will encounter it for as long as we live. Acquiring effective resolution skills for ourselves and then teaching them to our children is crucial for winning the battle on mental health.

I had bullied myself, and as a result, my personal dialogue became my daughter's voice. She then experienced bullying in her sphere. She felt inadequate and punished herself. When I noticed my child imitating my own frailties, I made a point to deal with my issues and then show her how to resolve inner and outer conflict in a healthy manner. This set her up for mental-health wellness and provided her with the confidence to tackle future problems. It also established trust between parent and child.

There was an incident when a student in my daughter's grade two class was taunting and gaslighting her. I was stunned that at seven years old, this boy was already playing a part in violence against women. My daughter felt safe to share this experience with me, which is a major win for me as a parent. We can only deal with what we know, and children need to feel confident at home if they are to express what is happening in their world. After I held that sacred space for her, I didn't send a nasty email to the school and blast the kid. Instead, I used this as an opportunity to learn more about the situation by initiating conversation with the school. I wanted to understand the other side and convey that we were experiencing an issue. By maintaining a calm and open approach, I was able to facilitate finding a solution while in a neutral place, void of hostility and tension. The teacher took us seriously and went to the principal right away. Discussions with the boy transpired, and this led to conversations on how to deal with subtle abuse. He did apologize to my daughter but when she came home, she expressed that his apology didn't feel sincere but was rather just a means to get out of trouble. My daughter and I therefore used this as another learning opportunity. Just because we set our intention to find a resolution to the conflict doesn't mean the other side will take accountability. Nevertheless, I showed my daughter how to communicate through a problem. I had her back and ensured she felt supported. We tried. We didn't allow a bully to continue the cycle. He might have not learned much from the experience, but my daughter sure did. He didn't bother her anymore because we held the line that her boundaries and mental health would not be messed with. This is how we establish healthy lines: we lead the way and our children become co-pilots of their mental health.

Bullying plays a large part in the mental health of a child, but it isn't the only thing. When any person is struggling with mental health, there's an undertone of a lack of identity.

We experience a low that mimics the darkness of the abyss. When this happens, we feel an absence of purpose in our own lives. Nurturing the exploration of one's identity in your home will benefit the mental health factor immensely. Every person (including every child) has a unique purpose on this earth. We are made with a one-of-a-kind identity that commands us to validate and honour our individuality. How do we solve the identity crisis with our kids? We begin by discovering our own purpose and modelling what that looks like for our young. Walking out our destinies is a personal mission. We can't manufacture purpose for our kids. We lead by example. I think this mentality flows nicely to the helicopter or lawnmower parent analogy. "Helicopters" hover over their child in an overprotective and intrusive way and the other "mows down" any hurdles their child might encounter.

Personally, I find it challenging to balance giving my child space while still teaching her how to navigate the world. I don't want my child to suffer or feel pain. I don't want her to struggle. But through roadblocks and toil, our children learn grit and problem-solving techniques. We must let them struggle to a point, but through it all they need to know that someone is behind them supporting them. They are not abandoned when they do require support. When my child is experiencing conflict, I must fight the "mama bear" urge to shut down the conflict. If I take over, she loses the opportunity to develop her own mental-health tools. She would only learn to rely on others to solve her issues. To create good citizens, we must educate our young on how to overcome barriers self-assuredly. Aim to be the "lighthouse" parent: a guiding light in storms showing the route to resilience and independence.

This parenting style nurtures purpose and identity in the child. At the very crux of positive mental health is knowing oneself and what is required to hold the line of self-love and respect.

We can all be challenged with mental health matters, but when we are committed to loving, respecting, and healing our identity, we can take profound steps to achieve those goals. This commitment is an internal guide that never fails. This is what our children need. This is what we must do for ourselves to ensure it for them.

Establishing mental and emotional wellness in the home is the greatest way a parent can show their love for their child. Since we cannot give what we don't possess, we have to face our fears and unmask ourselves to be capable of giving that precious gift of wellness to the mini versions of ourselves. Our inner healing creates healing pathways for them. Talk is cheap and kids, like skilled lie detectors, easily detect empty words. We must demonstrate with actions.

My mom has been an educator for over forty years, and she shared a tip that has always resonated with me when teaching kids: *I do. We do. You do.* The teacher models the action. The student does it with the teacher. Then the student does it confidently on their own. This method can be applied by parents teaching mental-health wellness to their children. It starts with the parent modeling positive mental-health coping strategies. The kids organically learn healthy inner thought processes which can then be applied to their communications with others. Being mentally healthy during childhood leads to reaching developmental and emotional milestones and learning healthy social skills for years to come. We have the power to alter generations of "poor feeds" and establish new ones that create healing, love, and empowerment. They will be able to cope with whatever challenges come their way and have an inner resolve to be resilient. Mentally healthy children have a positive quality of life and can function well at home, in school, and in their communities. *I do, we do, you do* changes the atmosphere.

GUIDING & REROUTING

Raising children is by far the most difficult job in this world and the most crucial one as well. Mother Teresa's moving words show us just how essential a healthy home is to create a healthy humankind. "And so, my prayer for you is that truth will bring prayer in our homes, and the fruit of prayer will be that we believe that in the poor, it is Christ. And if we really believe, we will begin to love. And if we love, naturally, we will try to do something. First in our own home, our next-door neighbour, in the country we live, in the whole world."[1] Love has many forms and requires flow from all angles to work properly. We can't just love with support and uplifting words; we as parents also must lead with wise counsel, discipline, and leadership. We aren't here to just be a friend to our children. We have a responsibility to guide them. This demands parents to step into various roles that facilitate children becoming the best versions of themselves.

I don't like the word *correction*. I don't believe in harsh punishments and withholding love to manipulate my child into acting a certain way. My husband and I focus on connection instead, which establishes a remarkably accurate internal GPS for our daughter. We teach her about triggers and how to self-regulate. We demonstrate how we control the narrative and possess the power to change the direction of our thoughts and actions. We are human and we will experience various emotions and react, but we are ultimately in charge of the direction our life takes. Parents are the initial Google Maps voice for their kids. When parents and guardians model healthy comms systems and gently reroute their children in the early stages, those kids learn to trust their own internal systems and soon take over the controls.

When we talk about being a role model for our children, we can't shy away from the discipline topic. Although most humans hate dictatorships and totalitarian systems, many still believe we need to operate with harsh punishments when it comes to disciplining our children. Yet it is possible to guide, mentor, and reroute our kids' behaviours without damaging their spirits and our relationship with them. We must create a haven for honesty first. We can't expect our kids to admit their fears and wrongdoings to us if the truth isn't safe. Separating the crime from their worth and identity is essential. Their actions maybe wrong, but they themselves are not bad. When we can set that kind of tone in the home, we create a shelter for trust. When our children can count on us with confidence, they will open up and confide in us—even when they have made a poor choice. They trust they won't lose our love over the admission. We have an obligation as parents to teach them that yes, there are consequences to their choices, but our love is unconditional.

Truth was always dangerous for me. I learned quickly that the fake lie kept me in the "worthy" column. Every time I was truthful, the punishment was amplified, and I never seemed to earn back approval. Lying became my friend. I could control the lie and the outcome of it. Telling the truth carried too much risk. It took me until my mid-thirties to kick the lying habit. I didn't want my child to grow up thinking the truth is unsafe, so I built up her trust by not overreacting to her missteps. I must be an anchor and a beacon for honesty. My husband and I reinforce that owning the truth might come at a cost, but it will never withdraw our love. Yet sometimes we struggle in this, so time and again we reconfirm to her the unbreakable trust bubble in our family. If we overreact and break that faith, we sever communication lines. If we can be the keepers of honesty, we remove the negative charge of the confession. With this, we create an understanding and acceptance of natural consequences.

Being an intentional influencer for our children is an exceedingly tough task. It requires parents to be almost superhuman. We don't always get it right with ourselves or with our kids, but when intention collides with determination, we do create a healthy environment in which they grow. Even with our commitment, I realize our kids won't always respond appropriately. It's like kids are put on this earth to test us and the very boundaries we set out for them. Though we establish borders to protect them, they need to investigate and experiment for themselves. I used to get really upset and annoyed my child would test the limits. At times I felt she was leading a mutiny and my feisty side would meet it with resistance. The more she tried to manipulate me, the angrier and more frustrated I became. This tug-o-war of emotions wasn't working. I had to take a step back and re-evaluate my approach. I get triggered by manipulation tactics because I was in multiple relationships and friendships where I got played like a fiddle. Now when my child tries these same moves, I immediately feel charged. In that moment I must talk myself through it. My daughter isn't those people. She's a kid just being curious and exploring the essence of boundaries. Her internal systems need to establish those lines. She needs to know which ones protect her and which ones can be bent or crossed. Realizing that children cannot collect this data or arrive at a proper conclusion without experimenting, I disarm my charge when she tests me. I choose to look at it from a different viewpoint. Now I am excited when she tests me both because it gives me an opportunity to grow as an adult and a parent but also because it's a gift for her. She is collecting data and reconciling it. That's what we want for our kids.

My dad once told me love is spelled T-I-M-E. What we invest into a relationship is what we get out of it. Parents needs to spend time loving their children in the ever-changing way they need it. Love also equals discipline. If we didn't care, we would never try to guide. The continual rerouting, instruction, and mentoring establishes values, morals, and an internal compass. Allow kids to question the why. Grant them the time and space to inquire about the moral lines of life. Questions are not disrespectful. They are safe and necessary for creating strong signals and developing an inner GPS. Even when our kids question their penalties, we must still hold the line on discipline because that is LOVE. I know how difficult it is to stick to a boundary when kids are crying and saying things that sting the heart. The guilt rises and we are tempted to go easy on them this time. We cannot trade our guilt for their consequences. Humans learn how to get what they want based on reactions and outcomes. Kids are no exception. They test. They observe. They weigh the risk. They push and push and push. They are seeing how important one rule is against another. If we work hard on the connection piece in the conflict with our kids and they feel safe, but we waiver on the penalty for such behaviour, we have taught them that particular boundary isn't important. We have modelled it's okay to disrespect people in authority over them.

Parents, we can't continue this. We must hold space, create safety, and confirm the negative effects to poor choices. Love is demonstrated in the time we put into the art of discipline for our children. They will grow up with a moral compass that points due north when it comes to accountability for one's actions. They will respect their leaders, teachers, elders, and humankind. They will evolve into good citizens who make conscious and wise decisions because they comprehend the magnitude of outcomes. Testing and questioning are to be welcomed, but our kids do need to accept responsibility. The point isn't to just punish them, but rather to reroute the destructive behaviour into positive changed actions. We mustn't cave to our kids' resistance to discipline. We owe them more than to let them continue the cycle of deflecting and throwing temper tantrums. No more negotiating with little terrorists. No more leaning on the excuse that we are tired. When we are faced with the internal-conflict guilt trip, we need to pose a question to ourselves. Do we love our children enough to dedicate time for effective discipline?

PLUGGED IN

Often life is a battleground, and mere survival is what we as parents focus on. When we are in that mode, it's difficult to always be present for our kids. My words aren't meant to chastise anyone but rather to sound the alarm of the gravity of the subject. We aren't going to be perfect, but if we can set the intention to try our best, day in and day out, we will be a plugged-in parent by definition. We need to calm all the noise and get into the game. We can't be bystanders who catch the highlights of our kids' lives. We need to be the engaging coach and razor-sharp referee who blows the whistle on ourselves and our children. We need to stop the narratives and actions that take us on destiny detours—for ourselves and for our future generations.

You know how sometimes when you watch sports, it feels like the referee isn't even watching the game? We are the referees of our own lives, but we've completely been blinded to the harmful infractions happening in front of us. This creates foggy filters and lenses towards how we see and interact with our children. We need to own our role as parents. We are our children's guides, mentors, referees, cheerleaders, and heroes.

To put this another way, we are all essentially lights. We all have the ability to shine. And as parents we not only have the responsibility to make sure we have our own lights plugged in and shining bright, but we also must ensure our kids are plugged in. We are in essence the extension cord for our children. Our children can plug in to other sources, but the reach is so much greater when it comes from their own tribe. Being connected, open, and vulnerable with our kids allows them to feel the love and connection which fuels them to succeed in life. We are the connectors.

Another way to safeguard our connection with our kids is to maintain our passion for life itself. We need to model *Know Thyself* and know that our identity is worth fighting for. This carves out a pathway for our kids to follow and discover their purpose and identity. Mediocrity is a silent killer and is the enemy of connection. Some of us have been through challenge after challenge our entire life, and after feeling so bogged down and lost, we fall. We lose our will to navigate through the maze. We find a zone in which we can hit auto pilot and we coast.

Benjamin Franklin is attributed to have said, "Most people die at twenty-five and don't get buried until seventy-five."[2] He was talking about emotional death. We are a culture that just goes through the motions and literally becomes the walking dead. We cannot let fatigue disconnect us from ourselves or our kids. You're not tired. You are just uninspired. We need to unearth things that breathe new life back into us. We require inspiration to fully experience what life has to offer.

Have you ever noticed the whole world is on a diet? I think when we deprive our physical bodies of nutrients, energy, and life for so long, we end up starving our souls as well. We need to take ourselves off the point-plan and regain our appetite for life so that our young may be inspired. When we have purpose, our children want to emulate that kind of passion and zest in their own lives. This is the greatest gift we can give them. Contend for excellence in your family. Fight for the people you love to live out their calling. Comfort zones and mediocre attitudes aren't living. Motivate your kids to be earth shakers and world changers by setting the example.

We don't need to be famous, powerful, perfect, or wealthy to lead our kids; we influence them through our enthusiasm for life. When I become the leader of my own life, a ripple effect of empowerment and motivation touches all those around me, including my daughter. Being a leader is not a title; it's a way of living. We must model grit and the attitude of no quit. Brave honesty and humility create a connection which allows the communication systems to desire the plugin. The story of the oyster and the pearl perfectly demonstrates what being a leading parent means. When an oyster is invaded by a parasite, it doesn't clamp down and avoid the problem. It does the opposite. The oyster welcomes the attacker and draws it in. It understands without the grit, there can never be a pearl. The oyster shows the power of resiliency by coating the parasite with a special liquid over and over, day after day until it turns its pain into a pearl. Just like the oyster, a parent can't shy away from the sword. A leading parent forges ahead with sheer will and a resolute spirit. A leader gets gritty when they encounter the grit of life. A leader is born when they recognize a battle is the conduit for bravery. This conscious conduct reverses the *do as I say, not as I do* mentality. We now show the way through life rather than just tell it.

Parent-led vulnerability, candidness, and honour forge trust with our kids. They need to trust us to be truthful about our own frailties and flaws. Trust is at the heart of being plugged in. They need to see us err, then observe how we work through our struggles. If we show them fake perfection, we teach them that they can't trust us with their own mess ups. Our connection and vulnerability become the birthplace of their resiliency. Establishing connection with our children generates healthy communication lines. When these lines are defragged and functioning at optimal levels, then parents can decode their offspring and act with wisdom. We can detect what they are saying beneath their outburst and undercurrent of heavy energy in the atmosphere. No matter what our kids say or do, we must hold onto this vital point: they are not seeking attention, they are seeking connection. They aren't screaming for isolation like their words might reflect, they just don't know how to articulate their pain. Therefore, parents need to read between the lines and become expert decoders.

When children develop eating disorders, they are feeling they have lost control so are taking control of the intake of food into their bodies. When young ones say their stomach hurts, they aren't trying to get out of going to bed, they are telling you they have anxiety about something. When they yell and have tantrums, they are finding too much chaos around them and they don't know how to stop it. When they hit and have episodes of rage, they don't know how to channel or release the fire within. When they seem nervous or timid, maybe they are in a situation that makes them feel unsafe. When your kids try to hurt you or others, this is a sign they are hurting deeply inside. When you see them obsessing or being excessive with something, they are trying to numb themselves through that compulsive behaviour.

When we attempt to drown our traumas, pains, and struggles with alcohol, exhaust them with exercise and starve them by withholding food, we model toxic coping methods to our children. Same goes with our OCD cleaning behaviours, our overaching work habits, and trying to validate our worth through relationships. These suppressive actions sever communication lines, and then the false identities begin to pop up. We stop the identity theft by intentional connection. Dealing is feeling. Once we process things, we discover the light. We become the change we wish to see by lighting the path for our children and blazing the trail for them. They then learn the skills to forge new paths and carry on the torch for their children. When they are lost, we need to guide them through the MAPP:

First, sit in the Mess with the child. Don't avoid it. Don't shove it under a carpet. Don't dismiss it. Don't devalue their experience. Messiness is uncomfortable but necessary to the healing process.

Next, help them find Acceptance. When we can accept what we cannot change, we release the hold the emotions have over us. We need to do a reconciliation within. Can we change this situation right now? It's a yes or no answer. If our child can change the outcome, great; teach them how to take steps to change their course. But if they can't, then they need to learn acceptance. This is difficult for most adults, but this is the linchpin to becoming a Captain Communicator at a young age. Acceptance releases the tension. Acceptance makes room for our central nervous system to calm down and reach a neutral idle. This doesn't dismiss the emotion; it merely allows us to continue with life in a rest and digest mode rather than trigger mode. It is safe to co-exist with our problems.

The third stop on the MAPP is channeling the Passion. Anger is just unfiltered or misplaced passion. We need to teach our kids that losing ourselves to anger and excessive passion does not demonstrate love for ourselves. Help them to find and pursue what lights them up, that they may live with renewable energy.

Finally, we need to change our Perception, not the image. If we can't change the outcome, we need to change how we look at it. Establish how looking at the situation through a different angle can help us learn resiliency, patience, maturity, and compassion. They will follow the leader because we become the hero they want to be.

CHAPTER

5

PEEPS

CONSCIOUS CONNECTIONS

I have a love-hate relationship with friendships. For as long as I can remember, I've struggled to find someone who loves me as much as I love them. Time and time again, my tender heart has been broken by friends who turned into foes. That rejection played into the narrative from previous hurts that I am not loveable even on a level of camaraderie. When I began the quest to unearth my true identity, I had to confront my fear of friendships. I needed to challenge the mentality that these pals should be forever. Some aren't. Most of the time certain people cross your path for a specific purpose and have an expiration date. I consider myself a lifer with my love, so this was a hard pill to swallow. When friendships petered out, I needed to look at them with appreciation for what they were and not with distain for the fact they ended. Just as with relationships, the friendships weren't all bad and I could always find something positive to take away. I'll admit though in the past I didn't choose my friendships, I just took whatever I could get. Yes, some people pop into our life like an epic movie scripted "meet cute," but we still control whether we cast them as a regular in our storyline.

When I realized I had the power to deny toxic companions, things shifted for me. I set an intention for conscious connections. No longer am I the victim of circumstance regarding friendships. I decide. I choose. Not everyone that comes into my life is meant for confidant status; some are just acquaintances—and that is okay. We need to be selective and choose wisely the ones admitted into our inner circle. One size doesn't fit all, but we should be brave and try on a new friendship. Just like when clothes shopping, we just put back the ones that don't fit. There's nothing wrong with those outfits, they're just not for me. The same logic applies to adding a new pal to our circle.

After vetting our new acquaintances and welcoming them into our sacred friend zone, setting early parameters and boundaries are vital for a healthy friendship. Honestly, I don't think I have ever done that. I'm a people pleaser and I struggle to set the margins right off the bat. But I realize it's better to do it in the beginning than try to backtrack it later. This guide or reminder is just as crucial for me as it is for you.

Having boundaries doesn't mean we are to come off as a dictator and list off a bunch of rules to be our friend. It means having open, sincere, and vulnerable conversations that establish the communication rules of engagement. We can't have clear transmissions if the two people are speaking on two different channels. Can you imagine the mutual benefit if we all agreed at the beginning of every budding friendship or relationship to set the proper frequency and tone and commit to showing respect in how we communicate? The fights, miscues, resentment, hurt feelings, and misunderstandings would be drastically reduced. When I meet a new person, I commit to getting to know them and to nurturing a bond. I organically mention that I am a softy and I wear my heart on my sleeve. This gives them the indication that I'm not a rough and harsh type of personality. I need a little cream and sugar with my coffee and conversations. From there I get to know them and ask questions and learn what their personality type is. I also try and ask them what their love language is and their preferred way to communicate. Do they send and receive better over in-person interactions, or over email, texting, or phone calls? Through such questions, I learn how I should conduct myself and on what channel they need me to meet them so they can feel safe within our relationship.

A friend of mine once texted a message saying how they felt sorry that I was going through a rough time and asked me how they could best support me through it. I thought that was the most loving thing someone could say to me. How incredibly considerate. They were even willing to switch channels just to show me how much I mean to them. We need to get to that juncture of commitment with our friends. Ask questions. Be brave enough to express what you need out of the alliance. Come to a mutual understanding of respect and operate with a code of conduct that reflects each other's core values. That is the greatest gift you can give.

Building a circle of trust and respect in a friendship takes time and effort. This is done by being vulnerable and genuine. I have a natural bend to be vulnerable and create a safe space for others to be vulnerable. This wasn't always the case though. In my twenties and early thirties, I was the master of masks. I never let people see the real, imperfect woman staring back at them.

I was scared they would think less of me if I was raw and real with them. If we approach relationships armoured up, they can only remain surface level. The deeper we go with someone, the closer we grow. When attempting the vulnerability factor with a friend, approach it like a layered cake and not a tidal wave. Find the balance to avoid oversharing in an effort to connect. Revealing too much information too soon may turn off new connections. I intentionally share something a little personal to see how that person responds. Not everyone can be trusted with your vulnerability or is even in the right space to handle it. This is why you offer little hits of it. Did they respond back with their own sign of unmasking? If they didn't, then you weren't too personal. Or perhaps they weren't ready yet to share or maybe they don't wish to go deeper. Being vulnerable is an art. Just like works of art, beauty is in the eye of the beholder. Some people might not appreciate the artistry of your vulnerability. If they don't want a deeper connection, that's okay. You can achieve that elsewhere or simply leave space for the possibility. However, if they remove a piece of armour and expose themselves to you, that's when trust is first established. They felt safe enough to trust you with that information. This is a treasure you guard with your heart. Each time you meet, you offer another layer of vulnerability, and they contribute a tier as well. Over time you have built a strong connection bonded by the power of naked vulnerability. This sets the tone for humbling truth and trust in the friendship.

Once we have established trust, we have paved the way for wholesome and nourishing communication within the friendship. If we could always be daringly vulnerable with our needs and share how we best send and receive signals, we would have highly functional communication transmitters. To sit down with a friend and map out how we envision the dynamic of that connection is an extraordinary firewall system that will protect the relationship. By forming "rules of engagement," we remove the probability of hurt feelings and disappointment from unmet expectations.

I often hear of and have personally experienced one-sided efforts when it comes to texting or calling a friend. In many friendships I am the initiator, in both the contact and of the making of plans. When repeated over and over, resentment builds and a lack of feeling valued forms. From some friends, I have had to disconnect and give space for them to maybe one day meet me in the middle. Some have reached out and others haven't made any effort. That's okay. This is a learning opportunity on how to love yourself and hold the line on a mutually respectful relationship. I have had to put some people into my grace category. These connections are made up of people that probably need extra love and support but who aren't necessarily close friends. I have removed the distain and resentment and just approach those relationships with a heart space that they need my love more than I need theirs. Generally though, if people want to enter a friendship with me, then the texting, calling, and connecting needs to be give and take. And we need to challenge ourselves to be upfront about expectations and what that looks like in each specific relationship.

We don't tend to be proactive in setting the parameters; rather, we stay quiet trying not to rock the boat, but stew about the grievance in silence afterwards. This is where friendships disconnect. Resentment and bitterness are poisonous in relationships. They are a virus that infiltrates the entire inner workings of a connection and then eventually the system will crash, and the friendship experiences a shutdown. Unless sincerity, ownership, and effort follow, there will never be a healthy reboot. There have been times where a friend has been upset with me over something and I had no clue as to what it was. For instance, one woman ghosted me for six months and I tried to find out what was wrong. After I flat out asked, "Did I do something to hurt you?" she finally replied that she was so angry with me she couldn't talk. This isn't healthy or fair. I'm still not sure what happened. We never had a disagreement. When there is conflict within friendships, we should show respect by facing the issue and giving the other side an opportunity to make it right. If we don't make room for amendments or at least discussion, we are in essence saying we don't value the connection.

Ghosting is immature. We need to become the driver and steer the course of our friendships in the direction we want versus giving up when things get rough or waiting so long that the water goes under the bridge. I used to allow that passive behaviour; now I don't. Our friendship can move forward when we both take accountability and try to make it right.

Or, if this is not possible, I am brave with the breakup and face it head-on. This is being conscious with our connections.

FRIEND FACTS

Maintaining a friendship is just like gardening. We sow seeds, we nurture, we weed, we water, we provide warmth, and we have a desire to see our seeds bloom. It takes all those things to grow a strong connection. It demands incredible effort to keep them alive. I'll be honest, I don't have a green thumb and plants and flowers commit suicide in my very presence, but I am an expert gardener when it comes to cultivating companionships.

I love deeply and I'm committed to seeing my budding relationships mature and grow. Tending to friendships requires a consistent intent to not let them wither and die. Every day I take a moment to think about the people in my life and appreciate them, and then when someone pops into my head, I initiate contact. What good does it do to just cherish someone in your own mind and never tell them? We must voice how much we value them. So, I make it my mission to text or call people the moment they cross my mind. I want them to know that I love them enough to put the effort in. Even when I'm busy, sick, or tired, I carve out a minute to let them know I care. Since every connection needs a different level of nurturing, I chat with some friends every day and others maybe once every six months.

Friendships are vital to one's journey. We cannot survive without companionship. If connection is the heartbeat of humankind, then we must continually ask ourselves how good our green thumb is when it comes to our friendships. Could we do better? Sometimes when we feel a disconnect or have conflict in a friendship, we are inclined to end it by uprooting it and throwing it away. We don't do that with our plants and flowers. We see if the pH in the soil needs adjusting. We give it more water. We put it in the shade or expose it to the sun. We provide it with special food. We try to bring it back to life. We need to apply the same logic to our friendships.

The practices of weeding and pruning in gardening and friendship are essential to growth. I've always thought pruning to be a strange concept; cutting away portions of the very thing you want to grow seems counterproductive. It's the opposite though. If we want healthy friendships, we can't ignore this process. It isn't easy and can be painful, but I come back to the question. What atmosphere are we committed to with our relationships? Do we value them enough to pick up the pruning sheers? Sometimes that relationship just needs some attention and a little TLC. Other times it might require difficult conversations and addressing things to mend the disconnect. Then there are also times we need to weed out that friendship entirely. Breaking up with friends is hard to do. I am still a work in progress in that area. I am never the one that thinks we can't be friends. I want to work it out and compromise. I'm a fixer. As I have matured, I've realized sometimes these connections are hurting me more than healing me. They take and take and take and never contribute. At some point you must love yourself enough to put an end to the robbery. It might just be a union that isn't serving you the best.

How do you define a toxic relationship? And a healthy one? I always go back to my 80/20 rule. We need to step back and reflect and look at the friendship from a different viewpoint. We will never agree 100 percent with anyone, including family and partners. If I generally align with 80 percent of a person, then I just accept there are going to be things and issues that fall into that other 20 percent, and I have grace for that. Knowing this, I try to be realistic when faced with conflict and I do an analysis. I ask myself queries and give honest answers. Does this person still align with most of my values? Do they contribute to the union, or do they just make withdrawals? Why do I love them? What's happening that is causing a disruption? Can it be addressed and resolved? Has the percentage shifted in difference of opinions and values where the balance is now a deal breaker for me? When we arrive at the answers, there's a yes/no decision to be made. Is this person still a true friend? If not, then we must weed them out. Often by their lack of effort or interest in reconnecting, they weed themselves out anyways.

What if, after all your work, you determine the friendship is worth saving but they have chosen to weed you out of their circle? This has been a tough one for me. I have been dumped a lot over the years and it's heart-breaking. I feel like it's an act of treason to the relationship itself that people are willing to just walk away rather than fight for our friendship. What I've learned though is they are not rejecting me or our friendship. They are rejecting the effort it takes to walk through the mud with me. It's hard work to do that. It takes two people willing to face the mirror and take ownership and accountability. It's easier to just dump and begin fresh with another person. The 80/20 rule is something to always reflect on. Are we willing to sacrifice a beautiful bond that is fulfilling and makes up that 80 percent to go on the search for that missing 20 percent? Because the next friendship will also have their own 20 percent of flaws and differences. Then there are times when them leaving is for your best interest even if you can't see it at the time.

I had a friend for fourteen years and we went through everything together. Just as when people fight side by side in wars and become a "band of brothers"—we had been a band of sisters. We also developed rare illnesses around the same time, which further bonded us because we knew what it felt like to fight for our lives. Looking back, our friendship shifted from healthy to damaging during that time of illness. We were "sick buddies" and were co-dependent on being in that sick energy. When I flipped the script one day and made a choice to work on healing, it uprooted the relationship. She turned on me and walked away from us. It broke me. It's a heart wound from which I still bear the scar. I didn't know how to handle the abandonment. At the time, that relationship was longer than the one I had with my husband. We had never had a fight. She just ghosted me. A year later I reached out again, and she responded. We chatted surface level stuff and soon she began to point out my flaws. Then, radio silence happened again. I didn't get the message, or was unwilling to accept it, so after my relentless attempts to work it out, she responded with hatred and told me to never contact her again. We've never spoken since. I went to therapy for months. It was a profound trauma.

Over the years, I have learned how to heal from that kind of rejection. It's been a journey for sure and I have had to move on. I discovered that for my own peace and healing, I can't look at that relationship with contempt and hurt. The end was bad but there had been more joy than sadness throughout. I appreciate what that friendship did for me. I think that to heal severed lines within, we must look for the good and find gratitude or if nothing else, a learning opportunity. Maybe she let me go so I could heal. Maybe she loved me enough to give me that gift because she knew I would never leave. Maybe she was too ill to shoulder the responsibility of our bond. I have sent messages over the years expressing my love and appreciation for what our friendship meant to me. I never received a reply, but I wanted her to know I valued the time we did have together. She recently passed away, and it's like I am going through the breakup all over again. I always held onto hope we would reconcile. Death is final. I can't fix this one. My last email was at Christmastime. I shared memories, photos, and pure compassion. I have no regrets. I tried. I loved. I gave it my all. I don't know why she pushed me away. I will never get answers, but I will love her forever even if she couldn't love me back.

My sweet Pam, there is no more pain, just love.

Laters,

me

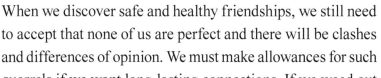

When we discover safe and healthy friendships, we still need to accept that none of us are perfect and there will be clashes and differences of opinion. We must make allowances for such quarrels if we want long-lasting connections. If we weed out everybody who disagrees with us, disappoints us, hurts us, betrays us, or angers us, we would have no one left. Everyone hurts another at some point, and that's why forgiveness is the only way to ensure continued connections. We also need to be realistic in the fallibility of relationships. No one can provide all that we need. Accepting the relationship for what it is, not what you wish it to be, is key. I have a wide range of interests and needs, and I caught myself trying to have deep philosophical conversations with some friends that never wanted to go there with me. They were fun and we had an amazing bond, but philosophy wasn't our dynamic. Then I had the deep-thinking group that I felt lacking in the fun factor. I ended up trying to change each friend to fit what I was wanting. I was wrong to do so. We need to accept people for who they are and love them for all they are or all they are not. We need to stop trying to change them to fit them into our mould of what we think that friendship should look like. Doing so builds resentment and frustration over time, and the once-deep connection develops cracks. Making room for people exactly how they are today is a sign of a deep respect and love. It's indictive of a person who has a healthy comms system in place.

All my life I had just desired people to make room for my quirky personality, my flaws, and my strengths, but then I realized I would need to do the same for others. This has changed the course of my friendships. They have blossomed because I accept them, value them, and celebrate them. I have grown my friend circle and I have made room for remarkable and unique people in my life, and they have made room for me. When I need something within a friendship, I go to the people that can fill my cup and if they can't be that for me, I know to go to another source. We must stop trying to get water from a dry well. Go to the well that will quench your thirst.

TOUGH TALKS

In any relationship or situation in life, conflict resolution is crucial. Of all the tools, wisdom, and education someone could acquire, that is the number one skill to have. If you can master the art of having tough talks with people to reach a mutually accepted solution, that's powerful. Ignoring, ghosting, or just walking away without any attempts to reconcile is rarely the answer. It takes courage to face someone, sit down with them, and hash it out. It's harder to avoid the problem when it's your partner and you live in the same house. But with friendships, I find it's trickier. For one, they didn't sign a contract to love you, so leaving you is simpler than a spouse wanting to end things. We aren't taught how to fight with friends or broach difficult conversations. In my experience when I have had conflict with a friend, we either broke up or we took an exceptionally long break and never dealt with it. We might reconnect months or years later as if nothing had happened. I loathe that approach. I would rather duke it out and reach an understanding. Then forgive and move forward. I am not passive-aggressive, just assertive in conflict. I want to face our issues head on—even if I'm in the wrong.

There was a time I made an inappropriate joke about Indigenous people in front of a friend. I didn't even think before I said it and she happened to be Indigenous. The energy shifted and we had an argument. I had hurt her. In the moment I tried to backpedal and say sorry, but I really didn't take ownership. We found a way to move to another topic, but I knew she was still upset. A few hours after reflecting on things, I texted her and apologized. We seemed to connect, and she accepted my apology. After that, I felt we were good. I had faced it and owned it. She was my friend. I don't try to intentionally hurt my friends but when I do, I must take accountability and rectify it. We don't talk regularly so I was thinking all was fine but, she hadn't forgiven me and stewed about it for months. When I saw her again, I knew things were off between us, but I had been sincere in my apology so I just gave her space to work through that. A little while later, she got stood up on a date and I happened to text her that night. I ran over to her place all dressed up and took her out on a date. We had a heart-to-heart, and she expressed how she had held resentment towards me and needed to work through that and knows I'm a good person with a good heart. She apologized to me for that. We had a tough talk and walked through conflict resolution. We forgave each other. It took time, but we did it. I'm proud of that. And I'm also thankful for that conflict because I've now been on a quest to check myself when I say things from a white-privilege stance. I no longer make those jokes, no matter who is in my presence.

As parents, we have another dimension to navigate within our own friendships when our kids have conflict with one another. How does one navigate mom-friend dynamics when our kids have issues with each other? It's hard to separate our children's fights from the parents.' We often take on our kid's grievances because "if you mess with my kid, you mess with me." It's so important to model how to resolve conflict so our children acquire the proper tools to disagree respectfully, take accountability, apologize, and forgive. I know most adults struggle with this so how can we expect the kids to do it? That's why it's imperative we learn it now. We are doing our children a disservice if we can't help them build a healthy comms practice when it comes to conflict. Most friendships with kids have a short shelf life. Sometimes they stay friends forever even throughout adulthood, but most of the time, their circle changes and evolves with each new grade they're in or activity they do. That's okay. Even if a connection cools down or ends, there's still a mature way to manage it. It doesn't do them any good if we just say, "kids will be kids" or "let them work it out themselves." True, kids act out and have conflict multiple times a day, but they don't yet have the tools to properly work it out.

A parent's job is to guide them. We need to get down on their level, address the situation, get to the root of the issue, and have everyone involved learn how to co-exist in a kind way. Then, if necessary, approach the other parents. I know this can be awkward and often when something is brought up about my daughter, I get defensive. I challenge us parents to sideline our egos in those moments and listen. Our perfect little angels can do wrong, and we have a responsibility to hear another parent out when an issue is brought up to us. This is especially delicate when it involves our own friends. I've seen close friendships end because of their children's dispute. To work through this—both with the kids and the parents—we need to commit to an atmosphere of resolution and not focus on just the conflict.

I find it a little humorous I am writing this chapter at a time in my life where I am facing this next point. It's been over two years in a worldwide pandemic, and everyone is pretty much done with it all. Emotions bubble up and surface in various pockets of our lives. Right now, it's affecting some of my friendships. We always say we can still be friends with opposing views and just agree to disagree, but that doesn't seem to be the case with COVID-19. I call it the Great Divide. We have been collecting data, feeding our belief systems, and now we have pledged allegiance to one of two sides—pro-vax or anti-vax. Who hasn't felt the fractures within their families and friends this season? We must find a way to stick together and love each other throughout our differences. We almost need a motto of "COVID Cannot Take Our Connections." We haven't been through this type of war before, and rules of engagement need to be agreed upon when approaching our relationships. By establishing a safe frequency in which to communicate with one another, we give room for our differences. Even before replying, saying the words, "I hear you" creates a secure line. These three magical words disarm the charge between people. Let's practice truly listening to what the other person is trying to convey. Doing this and accepting the words they say, even if we don't agree, permits information to filter through and reconnect the disconnection.

If we value and care about our connections, we must commit to resolving our conflicts. The problem with humans and communication these days is we love engaging in the conflict but loathe the resolution part. It takes courage, humility, dying to self, and grace. Conflict resolution is a pair. Looking at them as a unit, not separately, is how we establish healthy signals. We detect problems and then we work towards the fix. Granted, even after the effort is put in we might not reach a solution. Sometimes defragging includes replacing old wires and connections and installing new healthy ones. Ultimately though, we have no control over whether the other person will be devoted to working it out with you. But we do control our efforts. How committed are you to your relationships? Do you flee from any fight and become a ghost? Do you engage in a fight and have no thought process surrounding how this will play out? Once we commit to the conflict, only one of two things will happen—someone backs down, and peace can be found through discussion, or lines are severed.

When we enter a conflict, we should maintain awareness and realize the potential cost of our words and actions. We need to ask ourselves, "Is this worth it?" While we address issues, we still need to remember that we played a part in the breakdown. Can we express our frustrations without blaming or shaming the other side? Can we be accountable and take ownership? Laying down our ego and actively listening to what someone has to say, even if it means we might be triggered in the process, is the first step to moving through conflict. The next is making room within for the possibility that we might be wrong. This acceptance is a massive step towards resolution. We are not always right. It's not so cut and dry. Do you want to be right or have a friendship? Being right is overrated. Admittingly, it's difficult to swallow my pride and let the other person be right even if I could point out holes in their views. Yet, I would rather be wrong than lose a friendship. Granted there are boundaries and moments where we must weigh the issue, but we do need to own how we respond to the conflict itself. And when we have hurt someone close to us, let us be brave and apologize.

Apologies are undervalued in the conflict. How many encounters have we had that could've been resolved just by someone saying, "Sorry, I didn't mean to hurt you"? Apologize and forgive. This doesn't mean you forget, but you do let go of the attachment to the hurt. What are you loyal to more, the conflict or the resolution? If you don't forgive, you continue the conflict and there will never be peace. Your love for the bond needs to eclipse the anger from the offense.

BE THE BRASSIERE

Strong friendships only form because of the secure support each side gives. People all know how crucial a good fitting bra is for breasts to be properly supported. We need to start examining our friendships and provide that same kind of support for them. Be that comfortable brassiere that everyone looks for in the drawer. Every connection is different and unique, but we can be a pillar of strength in our own exceptional way to each friendship.

I wouldn't be here without my support system. Every time I experienced my miscarriages and health scares or when my life went off the rails, my friends showed up for me. They delivered meals, cared for my daughter, texted, called, took me out for coffee, sent flowers, and showed they love me. When there is no struggle, they are still there encouraging me and holding me up. I do the same because I find support in supporting others. When I formed Footprints: Infertility &

Pregnancy Loss Support Initiative, it was a challenge to get funding. I was feeling so discouraged and didn't know how I was going to get the funding. Then one day a friend called me and said she believed in me so much she wanted to give me two thousand dollars so I could birth my cause. I couldn't even grasp how someone could believe in me that much. She has been my rock in this project. More funds flowed after her contribution. Her support initiated an outpouring of reinforcements. People from all over the world surrounded me and held me up. Those friendships lift my life. How sturdy are your supports in your friendships?

Like I mentioned, we all have unique ways to show support. We don't need to give money to prove we back our friends, but we all can encourage and thus anchor the bond of friendship. I find it interesting how society has bought into some practices that show support and yet not others. Take wedding and baby showers for instance. All around the world, if you get engaged or announce a pregnancy, there is a guarantee a celebration of support will take place. But what about if someone never gets married or has children? Why don't we throw business showers every time a friend launches a new project or venture? Even sharing a post about a friend's business is support and it's free to do so. Giving a five-star review is a sign of pure patronage. Times have changed and we are in a digital world, so why are we being stingy with our support online? It literally costs nothing to share a post, to write a review, or to refer a friend and yet most of us never do it. We need to put the *ship* back into *friendship*. A ship carries and helps us reach our destination. We cannot get anywhere in life without our friends and support system. They anchor and carry us. Getting into the habit of asking our friends how we can better support them and showing up for them each day will strengthen the communication lines within that sphere. By expressing what we need to feel supported and then sending out reinforcements to the other side, we connect the friend to the ship.

Part of fully investing in our relationships is addressing the significance of honour. We all have diverse core values with our friendships, but honour should be at the pulse of all of them. Without honour, we have nothing. I realize I am an extremist in many ways from my thoughts to my actions, but I don't think we can be respectable people, citizens, partners, or friends without a character that emanates integrity. Throughout the pandemic, I am learning people define honour in diverse ways. This is where the "Great Divide" takes place—a disconnect of the honour code. If we can't agree on the definition of it, how can we defend it? In any case, when we call someone "friend," we sign an invisible oath to defend them. This may not be applied to acquaintances or people you are merely friends with on social media.

This kind of bond is a heart connection and thus the stakes are higher. It carries a similar mentality as a mama bear: if you mess with my friend, you mess with me. I don't take my friendships lightly and when someone challenges or attacks my people, I pledge to defend their honour. It may be a subtle gesture, or it may involve taking a bullet for them, but the point is that I am in their corner. If each friendship included someone rooting for them, can you imagine the support in our lives? I see a lack of care in that realm. Taking a hit for someone is scary, but without putting money where the mouth is, what does that say about our own honour and character? Ask the people in your circle how they define honour. Enquire if they think you're an honourable friend. Let's reinforce the support systems by bringing back the honour code and reconnecting to the pulse of friendships.

Having a best friend doesn't always mean you have support. I truly hate the term "best" friend. It implies that this one is superior, and the rest don't quite measure up. We might be closer to one person than the next, but let's do away with the term *best friend* and instead replace it with *dear friend*. By labeling someone "the best" we are devaluing other connections. Kids feel hurt when someone in their class calls the person beside them their best friend. I have felt a bit rejected when that term is used in my presence. I don't need to call someone my best friend for them to know how much they mean to me. I don't need to announce it and make others feel less than. Let's just concentrate on creating and maintaining healthy bonds and focus on a the-more-the-merrier mentality. Don't close off your circle because you now have a few friends or a bestie. Expand the support system.

We need to challenge ourselves to step out and never stop making friends. We will never have too much support so why stop cultivating companions? Be the support to others. You never know if they have anyone else to lean on. I never want to shut someone out. I never want to say I don't have room for someone. Feeling excluded in friendship circles is the number one reason fractures and hurts happen. Let's build a firewall against those severed lines and be inclusive not exclusive. This is how we support the future of friendships. Be the friend you wish to have.

CHAPTER

6

THE 'RENTS

COMMUNICATION INCUBATOR

As vital as it is for us to safeguard a baby in a mother's womb, nurturing healthy communication pathways for our kids is just as crucial. They are born from a physical incubator but then enter an emotional one within a family unit. More focus, education, and importance need to be placed on the intention of forming sturdy transmission lines for our young. This chapter isn't to criticize us but to inspire us to do better for ourselves and our offspring. Children learn how to send and receive signals by watching their parents. From infancy and throughout their upbringing, our kids develop the foundation for communication that will impact every situation and relationship they face. If caregivers have acquired emotional intelligence and communicate clearly and effectively, odds are their children will too. Children form concepts and beliefs about themselves based on their environment, how their parents interact with them, and how their parents communicate with others. We are the model they will mirror. When parents are good communicators with their children, they demonstrate honour and integrity towards them. Children then begin to feel that they are heard and valued by their parents, which is a boost to self-worth. But if we haven't turned our own signals into superpowers, our incubator could hurt them. Negative exchanges can lead to children believing that they are insignificant or unworthy and that their feelings don't matter. This may create feelings of distrust, and if not resolved, a disconnection happens. We have a responsibility to ensure we have healthy comms systems in place to teach them to our kids. If we don't defrag and put firewalls in place for the entire family, we are the virus that will create a short in their feed for years to come.

How well do your parents communicate? Are your own signals superpowers or kryptonite? Think of every argument you've had with friends, family, bosses, or significant others. Were you able to articulate your needs and opinions with respect and receive feedback with grace? Or did you explode in anger and spew low-blow comments? None of us are going to be perfect, but we can all consciously work towards being great communicators. If we don't learn from our parents' and our own crashes, won't our children continue the faulty code we ingrain into them? Our parents all made mistakes and we will certainly err with our own kids, but isn't part of parenting trying to do better than our predecessors? Every day we learn more about mental and emotional health. Each year we are informed of better ways to parent and connect with others. We must start making ourselves accountable and put these new findings into our parenting practices. I want my child to be equipped better and earlier than I was. I want to set her up for success, and not have her be a victim of my lack of personal growth. It is widely accepted if a parent has difficulties with addiction, eating disorders, OCD behaviours, fears, anxieties, depression, and unprocessed traumas, their children are more likely to experience those very same issues. Parents can change the course of their lineage, but it takes work, commitment, intention, and grit.

For most of my life, I ignored and ran from my issues. Then I had an epiphany. I finally looked in the mirror and was honest with myself about my own crap. I learned that the only way to beat it was to go through it. Rumi famously said, "The wound is the place where the Light enters you."[1] The wound is the conduit to healing our systems and clearing a better path for our children. If we never peel back the bandages, irrigate the lesion, and provoke healing, the wound will spread to our children.

You are going to see me bounce around with perspectives in this chapter. As an adult with children, I am in an interesting situation when discussing communication and parenting. I have parents and I am a parent. Interacting with our parents and then with our kids creates remarkable and challenging parallels. I think we all want to emulate the good our parents did with their children and also commit to doing better with our own. As we embark on parenthood and personal development, we can get caught up in looking at all that our moms and dads did wrong rather than celebrating what they did right. We all have messy families. Dysfunctional transmissions happen everywhere, and perhaps that's something we need to shed light on. We envision what a family should be like and then we measure our personal dynamics against this unicorn ideal.

Every generation has built-in comms systems from their upbringing and their current environment. When we bring children into this world, they are the sum of us and our ancestors. Did my parents do me wrong with some things? Absolutely, but they also did me right. My brother and I have the kindest and most sensitive of hearts; that came from my parents. We are loving humans and are present parents to our own kids. We modeled that from our upbringing. I didn't need to be the change in that department. My parents did a lot of good with us despite their own unhealed wounds. I must give them credit for that. In a perfect world parents and children would have free-flowing transmission lines and when there is a short in the circuit, they come together and work out the problem and reboot to functional settings again. It doesn't work like that in reality. We are all flawed and have our own bugs to work out. But I've had to change my outlook on my parents' approaches.

For a long time, I solely focused on all their mistakes and the resulting impacts on me. I played the victim like a pro. But even though parents are responsible for that childhood incubator, once we grow up, with or without our parents' support, it's up to us to heal and make a better system for our own children. I choose not to be a causality of my parents' wounds. I make a conscious effort to accept their imperfections and praise their many successes. This breaks the cycle within and allows me to shift the trajectory for my daughter. Thanking our parents for the right they did us is healthier and more beneficial than blaming them for the wrong.

When we become parents, the communication incubator goes full circle. Our parents first formed a comms network that shaped our own practices, then we created an incubator for our kids, and now we must devise one for how we interact with our parents as adults. If we want to have a healthy incubator with our families, then we must commit to healing from the root. I had to forgive my mom and dad. I carried resentment for longer than I care to admit. If I released them, there wouldn't be anyone left to blame for my issues. We don't bring up past wrongdoings, but through my daughter I do see them try. They are phenomenal grandparents. I used to get jealous—how could they love her in an unconditional way and not me? They clearly have it in them. But then I shifted the lens I was looking through and chose to see them as knowing better now and making it right with me through her. I wholeheartedly forgive the frailties of my parents. I don't need them to verbalize their flaws. I only can heal myself and my family if I allow myself to let go of any wounds from my parents. I release the notion they should've known better. They couldn't do what they didn't know. When I fed mercy, healing, and forgiveness into the lines, I saw a reconnection take place. Some paths were closed forever but we found new routes to plug into. We rebooted our relationship, and I found my identity again. Forgiveness and mercy became the linchpins to the incubator. There will always be wounds, viruses, and crashes to navigate through. But if we can focus on constructing rather than destroying, we will ensure a healthy comms incubator for generations to come.

BOUNDARIES

Whether between parent and child or grown adults and their parents, boundaries are central to safe and respectful communication practices. Boundaries are behaviour guidelines that need to be valued and followed by each party within that comms bubble. We often talk about the importance of setting the margins but not so much on what to do if people violate them. It's more complex when it involves family, which is why it's all the more vital to establish healthy behaviours early on. If we all could know and articulate what is acceptable and what isn't, and then respond in rest and digest mode when someone crosses those limits, we would be Jedi Masters of communication. We need the "Set Up" before entering a conversation. Boundaries don't need to be brash; they just need to be clearly defined. Telling and showing my child what is expected from her when we have a dialogue is part of parenting. I model this in how I communicate with my husband and in how we converse with her. We tell her she needs to express her feelings and verbalize them to us. We don't yell in our house. We nurture a cone of safety to allow the words to flow. This is teaching her how to respect boundaries and set them for herself. I didn't have this until my late thirties, and it's been a work in progress to achieve.

Boundaries are tricky when you try to instill them after a relationship is already formed. I find it way easier to meet someone new and establish the expectations at the outset. With family, they know your history and the way you have accepted treatment during past conversations. It can be very messy when you try to flip the script after thirty-plus years.

I have failed miserably in my attempts to set healthy margins for myself while still respecting other people's boundaries, but I am committed to the journey. This is the key to bettering our sent and received messages. As an adult, I still find it difficult to approach a tough topic with my parents. My inner child wants to be the driver which causes the balance of power to be lopsided. The parent-pleaser in me wants to make an appearance, yet adult children ought to be equal with their parents. I still respect their authority, but no longer am I inferior. When I need to broach a hard conversation with my parents, I just set it up properly. "Mom and dad, I have something to say to you; I am not looking for approval or advice. I am happy with my decision, but I would like to share it with you and have your support." This has been a gamechanger for me and the way my parents receive my information. Instead of barking my demands to my mom and dad, I aim for connecting with them.

The process of setting boundaries needs to be realistic with our kids and with our own parents. No one is perfect. Everyone has unique needs and ways of communicating and we need to find a way to protect our rights in the dynamic as well as respect the rights of others. I go back to the 80/20 rule. Twenty percent of a functional relationship will have flaws and quirks, and I just have to accept that. But there's also 80 percent of flow and cohesiveness, so I am going to give grace for the little bit of dysfunction and focus on what is functioning well. There we enter a mutual understanding and are mindful not only of how to get our messages across in a loving way, but also of how to receive them without falling into the trigger trap. To ensure we aren't the victim or aggressor, we must know how to set healthy emotional, mental, and physical boundaries in relationships. This shapes a sort of Charter of Rights for communication. What are our rights? We must identify them with every communication bubble and then work together to follow them. These are the rights I have created, and they are universal for everyone.

It is my right to be in a safe environment.
It's okay to establish boundaries and have them respected.
I have the right to be heard and listened to.
My emotions, thoughts, and experiences are valid.
Even if we don't agree, verbal attacks will not be tolerated.
No means no.
I have permission to fully express what my core
values and needs are and have them met.
I am willing to compromise and find common ground.
I take ownership of my words and actions.
I will apologize when I'm wrong and
forgive when I am wronged.

This charter provides a secure space to connect and communicate—a neutral zone where information can be delivered and processed, and decisions formulated. A parent who repeatedly doesn't accept your "no" is violating your boundaries. When a loved one crosses these limits, communicate this with them and establish consequences. Protecting boundaries is probably the hardest part, and I still wrestle with how to execute it properly. If you also struggle with this, enlisting the help of a counsellor is wise.

When it comes to our kids, we also need to maintain the boundaries we set within that parent/child parameter. The child who continues to infringe upon the household charter of rights must face appropriate consequences. Otherwise, they will never respect you or people in authority. We truly teach people how to treat us.[2] I spent most of my life as a people-pleaser and never wanted my parents to be upset with me. I took a back seat in disagreements, swallowed my opinions (this is hard for a feisty girl like me), tried to be the peacekeeper, and apologized my way out of the slightest hint of trouble. However, my not fighting was hurting my relationship with my parents. I eventually would explode or just let things fester until roaring resentment poured out.

Disagreements are going to happen, so we must learn how to fight wisely and pick our battles. Conflict is healthy and is the pathway through which we set boundaries so that everyone can feel safe. Whether the argument is a full-on brawl or a little spat, conflict is the way we say, "You can go this far with me, but no further." Until we are confident in creating and holding these boundaries, we never truly demonstrate the love and respect we have for ourselves or the relationship. But the same goes for showing the self-control and discipline to not engage in a fight. Shrewd communicators will fully express themselves in a healthy way and still know when it's best to remain silent.

Just because I learned how to fight in a better way doesn't mean I engage in conflict every day. I can accept and let go of certain things and I can also identify what my dealbreakers are. I share these in a non-combative way with my parents and just tell them, "When you do or say this, I feel _____."

Or when they have clearly upset me, I respond with, "What you said made me feel triggered and not respected, is that what you intended?" I ask for clarification before waging an all-out war. Conflict management is so vital because most of us don't know how to communicate when angry. Many either withdraw and go silent, become a doormat, freeze into a pillar that cannot process any coherent thought, or explode like a volcano. Even if you don't react this way, other people will. The only way through it is to learn the art of managing conflict.

Don't shy away from a disagreement. Face it with humility and emotional intelligence. Learn what your core values are and create a boundary around them. Protect them without issuing a counterattack when the lines are crossed. Create an inner dialogue before initiating a war with your parents. Is this a bad day for me? Is it a bad day for them? Is there a way to say this and find a way through it, or is it a moot point? Is this a tiny issue or one of my core values? Pick your battles. By doing this, you strengthen the comms system in your family unit and find clarity around the bigger issues that need addressing. We don't want to always be in fight mode. We enter a war when we feel wronged or hurt, and can end up cutting the feed further. Instead, we need to shift our focus and manage the conflict so we can resolve it.

If you don't have healthy personal boundaries and uphold the charter of rights for communication, setting parameters with the in-laws could prove to be difficult. I didn't have any communication strategies when I was first married. I went to my default mode of not wanting to rock the boat. I wanted to impress my husband's family and not make them angry. This again is a faulty tactic, because usually over time, my emotions spilled over and caused an eruption. Melding two people and their families together is probably the most unnatural thing I can think of. Sometimes it's cohesive and people get along great, but other times it can be very tense. I didn't always understand why the friction would happen, but I have tried to see it from a different perspective. A person marries the love of their life. They are grown adults who are looking to carve out a life of their own, but the mom and dad have nurtured their precious child and have been the woman or the man of that person's life until now. It's like a changing of the guard or a passing of the torch, and I can see how that could feel like they are losing a part of themselves and a sense of control in a way. It's essential for couples to discuss the parameters of their relationship and how they see protecting those boundaries before getting married. Then they should come up with a plan on how to verbalize this to both sets of parents while still honouring the charter of rights for communication as a whole.

The biggest foe to the in-law dynamic is unclear expectations. The couple has ideals of how their families will interact with them as a married couple, and the parents and in-laws also have their own visions of how life will be. We all need to be candid about our expectations. We need to hash this out with our partners and be in sync with each other before going to our respective parents to set the parameters of the marriage. This initial stating of needs is another version of the "Set Up." This is a delicate task though because feelings can get hurt when boundaries are put in place. The receiving end can feel like they've been imposed upon with rules, and nobody likes rules. The in-laws might feel that they aren't needed anymore, which is not the case. Parents and families play a vital role in a couple's life, but they should be the supporting role, not the lead. Major decisions, parenting choices, careers, religion, politics, schooling, where to live, and the innerworkings of a marriage require zero interference or unsolicited advice from family members. We still need our parents but in a different way. We must have the space to flourish and even fall. Couples also need to appreciate parents have been around the block once or twice and could have valuable input. It's all about two-way respect.

More attention on this needs to be addressed before couples decide to say, "I do." We need to reassure our parents they aren't losing us. I have stumbled a lot when it comes to articulating my needs and wants with my in-laws, but I am committed to the process. I am dedicated to my husband, and I love him with all my heart. My love and my intention to hold the line on the charter of rights for everyone are gifts to myself and my relationships. I don't need to always be right or hold the power, I just want to connect. We are all on the same team. If we can get to that juncture, where our desire to win is overshadowed by the wish to move the team forward, there we embody connection.

HEALING

What I have learned when approaching communication with parents is humility will always activate healing. Whether we require restoration from the past or just want to ensure healthy communications going forward, humility is key. Just like how we need to tune the strings of a guitar or piano for a better pitch, being humble tunes the dialogue. When we are hurt, we transmit an unpleasant tone. I can resonate with this.

After my dad left and then returned, my sent and received messages were coming from a trigger mode. I would lash out in anger or interpret messages to be a slight against me. Anger is often just misplaced hurt. If we don't deal with our rage, it can morph into resentment and bitterness and cause all our words to taste bitter to ourselves and to the people receiving them. My resentment stemmed from feeling that my dad rejected me and that nothing I did could ever win his approval. This wasn't true. His departure was never about me, but my comms system continued that toxic narrative for a long time. I replayed this reel repeatedly for many years. It was the best-selling fiction that continued to cast me as a victim and my dad as the villain. One problem with this storyline was the victim role never helped me heal, and staying angry at my dad ensured a communication breakdown.

One day I was frustrated over an interaction I had with him, and I shared my irritation with my brother. He eloquently responded with encouragement to just show him mercy. That wasn't the response I was looking for. I wanted him to buy into my fiction and join in on the bitterness plot. He did the opposite. My younger brother disarmed me. I sat there staring at his text message and over the course of the day, I realized I had been approaching communication with my dad from a destructive space rather than a healing one. It was an epiphany. Ever since that day, I have adjusted my tone with my dad, and he responded immediately with a different pitch. It was magic. Mercy and humility towards my father were the catalysts to defragging and rebooting my internal communications system. I no longer write fiction. I swapped out the lens and I saw the true story. I let go of old scripts and learned how to forgive.

Once I began to show mercy towards my dad, the compassion melted both our hearts. We found a new place to connect. One of these new pathways was with my daughter, Lexi. As I mentioned before, I initially felt jealous of the connection my parents had with her. But their accountability and apology are shown in how they treat their grandchildren. I could continue writing the narrative of hurt and envy or I could interpret their actions as pure love. It's a do-over. To witness the relationship between Lexi and my parents has been incredible. They seem to have a secret language that emanates a kindred spirit. Their bond is inspiring to me. There is no hurt. There is no past. They just love and she meets them in that sweet place. I get to see my parents through a different filter, and I love it. The bond they have with her is igniting a stronger bond with me. Our relationships within the family unit are all linked together. When you connect on one side, the other automatically draws closer as well. I didn't have to force anything, I just needed forgiveness and gentleness to override the foggy lenses. Lexi is the bridge. Her given name is Alexandra. My husband and I appreciate the meaning of words and we desired our daughter to have a mighty name. Alexandra embodies influence. Her name translates to "defender/protector of man" and the "one who saves warriors."[3] She came into the world with a purpose to save. She is going to move mountains.

She already has by connecting to my parents' hearts and then linking the connection back to me. She is living up to her name. Thank you, my sweet one. Healing a childhood wound as an adult wasn't easy for me, but it was necessary. There were things I experienced that weren't my fault, but it is my responsibility to heal now. We all at one point in our lives have been a victim of circumstance but we ourselves are not victims. For the longest time I was caught up in repeating "Why should I have to do all this work when it wasn't my fault?" The thing is, that narrative doesn't serve us. It chains us to victim mode and stagnation. We cannot heal there, nor can we grow. It takes guts to dig ourselves out of that place. Healing is about looking beyond what is presenting in our lives. There's always a root cause to the hurt. Arriving at that point creates a sort of detachment from the suffering and self, and focuses on recovery.

The mother wound is intricate and multi-dimensional. The bond between child and mother (or whoever took care of us) makes up the foundation of our disposition, identity, and intuitive function. This connection began in the womb and had a powerful impact throughout our upbringing. If we didn't get properly nurtured growing up, that void affects us in every stage of life.

Father wounds are another strong influence. That relationship or lack thereof provides another footing upon which we build our identity. Abandonment by the father sends a shock wave to his child throughout their lifetime. The ripple effect of a father's rejection is palpable. This isn't an excuse to blame all our issues on mommy and daddy, but rather it gives us a portal through which to begin the healing journey. When we can identify where the problems began, we can work backwards to move forward. Sometimes we must investigate both relationships and try different filters. Who nurtured our parents? Did they have good role models or bad ones? How much inner healing have they done themselves? Their weaknesses as well as their strengths become embedded into us. A generational line and our environment have shaped us. When I see my parents through a curiosity lens instead of a judging one, I discover empathy. I am a parent now, and I realize I am passing down the good and the bad to my own child. With this awareness I cut myself and my parents some slack. We all need to own our decisions, our wins, and our fails but in the end, I chose healing over staying hurt.

To induce healing, the first step is to acknowledge that even though we might have issues, there's still a lot of good in us. This helps us look at the positives that came out of our DNA, parents, and ancestors. We are valuable, precious, and we aren't here by accident, so we can't be bad. Somewhere we were shown love and when we can get back to the root of love, we unearth healing. It's never too late to heal our history. Even if all we know is trauma and brokenness, we can be liberated and create new pathways of love and freedom. This builds a bridge to having healthy, nurturing, loving, and safe connections as adults. Sometimes healing the parent fractures is not realistic, but resolving our own wounds can change the course of our lives. Some upbringings may be unforgiveable, but this isn't about excusing poor parenting. This is about repairing, restoring, and reinforcing our communications systems and ultimately our very identity. This self-love gift will allow us to form other healthy maternal and paternal bonds in our sphere. The point is, we all need healing, and we all require connection. We all need love from family. Whether it's your bloodline or the people who make up your tribe, one's sense of community and commitment to that bond is essential. This isn't about anyone else; it's about freeing ourselves from the shackles of sorrow. We do this by deconstructing old ways to build new and stronger ties. If it's with your family or creating fresh connections, finding a new place to build from is essential.

I have an incredible relationship with my parents now because I found better lenses through which to see. Through my faith and "soul optometrists" I was able to look at my mom and dad with eyes of love. I pulled back the layers of hurt, rocked my messy vulnerability, injected love, discovered my super identity, and found inner healing. This activated a stronger relationship with my family. I am no longer co-dependent on my wounds. I choose constructive words and actions over combative ones. I swap out the hurt label for healed. I formed sturdy systems within, found sound ground for my relationship with my parents, and then reinforced the bond with my own child. I am a better woman, daughter, wife, and mother with these nurturing communication cornerstones.

REM STATE (RESPECT EMPATHY MERCY)

When we reach a point of healing and connection, we enter a REM state within our families (Respect, Empathy, Mercy). Just like during Rapid Eye Movement in our sleep, positive things happen within our relationships. The meaning of the acronym is different, but the results are the same: the brain exercises neural connections crucial to one's overall well-being and mental and physical health.[4] Our very health requires us to fight for a REM state. How do we do that with our parents? It is through a conscious daily intention to override our emotions and hurts. I choose REM state because I choose me. I hurt me when I hold onto hurts. When I practice REM with others, I inadvertently enter REM with myself. It's a boomerang effect. With this realization, I commit to *respecting* my parents in a new place that is safe for both of us, I choose new filters to see through so that *empathy* comes into focus, then I arrive at *mercy*.

Every encounter, conversation, and situation I experience with my parents is now from a deep healing place rather than a hurting one. I don't want tension, conflict, and suffering. I want to communicate and connect on a loving, mutual, and respectful level. We are not responsible for how others communicate but we are liable for our own exchanges. My relationship with my parents isn't perfect by any means but it is healthy. Leading with respect has allowed me to appreciate my parents more. It has gifted me room to learn, grow, and practice grace. The more I stay in REM, the more I heal. The more I heal, the stronger the connection becomes. I value this connection with all my heart, and I will continue to contend for it. Thank you, Mom and Dad, for meeting me in the *respect* space.

Once respect is established, we can move into the *empathy* space in the REM cycle. When we value an interaction and approach it with thoughtfulness, we open pathways for the willingness to understand. Empathy is sensing someone else's pain or seeing through their eyes. Empathy is also empowerment. It is a force that cuts through all the things we disagree on and brings into focus a picture of commonality. When we can truly step into the shoes of someone else and visualize walking in those shoes, the atmosphere shifts in the conversation. Empathy is oxygen, and the winds of change in energy help us see things from the other person's perspective. This doesn't mean we reach a consensus all the time but we do have an opportunity to appreciate their viewpoint. We can get there because we visualize ourselves looking through their lens. That is incredibly powerful.

So, when I broach topics with my parents, I lay the foundation of respect then speak with an undertone of empathy. Before even attempting a difficult conversation, I consider how they might feel my words and I play with my language to ensure I approach them with Tender Loving Care. Every time I have done the work to get to REM with them, our interactions have been successful. No fights. No hurt feelings. Just a beautiful exchange. They begin to empathize where I am coming from. Though I came from my parents, we are quite different in our views and way of living. Yet, somewhere in the REM space we reach a common ground. I encourage everyone to make empathy the goal, not winning. Discussions and debates should never be about winning or losing, but about learning, connecting, and deepening a relationship. Empathy is at the heart of it all. Empathy sparks compassion, and bridges the disconnection or disagreement.

Mercy completes the REM sequence and brings it all together. Respect and empathy are essential, but mercy matters most. It's mercy that invites forgiveness into the picture, and we all need forgiveness. Mercy is what connects us all together despite our clashes. Morphing into a merciful heart space enables true communication, reconnection, and reconciliation. It changes the approach from hard to soft. If we want love in a relationship, we must commit to mercy. Love is mercy. Yes, my parents hurt me, and I hurt them. But we all must decide what are we more committed to in that moment—the cut or the cure. If I only focus on the cut, I stay upset and the wound festers and grows. After a time, infection begins and spreads. The once little wound now takes over the whole relationship and resentment feeds the open gash. But when we apply mercy to the situation, we shift the attention to the remedy.

Like I said, we all need forgiveness. At some point, we are all going to hurt and cause a disconnection but part of being a Captain Communicator is acquiring tools to repair the disconnect quicker and better. Mercy is the ultimate utility tool for communication. When in doubt, apply mercy. It's a healing salve that will never let you down. The more you spread mercy, the more you grow the love. True love relinquishes ego and helps us move through offenses caused by the flaws of others. Mercy, humility, and intention are mighty connection protectors. They sustain the love when bonds otherwise would be severed. Without mercy in the mix, the annoyances and nuisances that impede relationships become strained and then disconnected. Mercy has freed my love. I no longer hold love for ransom. I often think of how I unintentionally mess up and say things out of turn. I require mercy all the time. So, if I do, others do too. Mercy is a two-way street.

When we enter REM state, it automatically calms the family dynamic even amongst occasional dysfunctions within. No family is perfect, but we can all aim for peace. This chapter is about improving interactions with parents and families, but only for those relationships that are healthy to pursue. I'm not speaking of toxic or harmful situations. Sometimes we can't fix our family tree. That is a tough pill to swallow when we must walk away. In those instances, put the REM into practice with others in your sphere and aim to achieve it with yourself even when you have to cut the feed with your parents. We all need REM state even if we find it outside our family unit.

"Being peaceful" tends to get the reputation that one makes peace with everyone. I disagree. Peace is about calming the chaos within and then allowing that calmness to subdue the storm in our outer worlds. Peace can mean detaching from contaminated connections. Peace is about action not inaction. Don't be a peacekeeper. Be a peacemaker. There is a stark difference between the two. Choose to create harmony with your parents or the people that are in your life who nurture you. Or choose peace by letting go of attachments to toxic parents. Get on board or get out; there is no middle when reaching REM state. It's about going all in and deep within.

REM is all about healing and we cannot heal if we are not protecting our peace. Family dynamics are complicated and challenging. We all want to be loved, approved of, and to fit in. Sometimes we don't fit. I am a person that never fits in naturally and have had to get good at making room for myself. We need that kind of logic when approaching parents and families. We must get away from seeking approval and move into connecting, understanding, and appreciating. All these tips help us to work out better communication strategies no matter the subject. We are the drivers. We control the narrative of our interactions. Even if the other side isn't willing to meet you, we are still the masters of our own messages. Aim for the REM and you will be surprised how the comms systems with your parents have a better flow of sent and received messages.

CHAPTER

7

OFFICE SPACE

SAFE PLACE

Communication within the workplace is another area that continually challenges me. Ever since my first job when I was sixteen, I have endured bullying, harassment, gaslighting, cattiness, exclusion, gender bias, and emotional or mental abuse. Most of my jobs became a prison instead of a paradise. People don't leave bad jobs; they leave cruel people. Why doesn't our society put a higher value on being safe in the workplace? We pay attention to protocols and procedures when it comes to physical safety, but we are still at the beginning stages of emotional and mental protection. In the last ten years we have seen an uptake in mental health awareness in the workplace, but I find it reactive rather than proactive. Programs are in place to aid us when we are struggling, but negative work culture needs attention to prevent or reduce the issues in the first place. Archbishop Desmond Tutu says it best. "There comes a point where we need to stop just pulling people out of the river. We need to go upstream and find out why they're falling in."[1] We need a complete overhaul of how we do business. We must make the office space a safe place. Can you imagine the creativity, collaboration, and solutions that would flow when the community within the business feels safe? We need leaders to care more about people than profit. What they don't realize is that the more they invest in the intangibles, the more wealth they will achieve on all fronts. Profit is a by-product of a safe, flourishing environment.

A big contributor to the perpetual cycle of unsafe working conditions is that we've been trained to think this is normal. We require more people to step out and speak up. Just because this has been a normal way of operating doesn't make it right. We cannot use "This is how we've always done it" as an excuse anymore. We first need awareness through education and then a commitment to evolve the atmosphere. Leaders must change their old ways and employees must elevate the standard. We can all see the unsafety in the work culture, yet our fear overrides our courage. If we all stood up and demanded our worth, fought for emotional and mental freedom, and banded together, we would establish a better system. We the people have the power to make improvements. We all have a leader within, we just need to demonstrate how big our braveness is. Safety is a human right. We must hold the line on being safe at work and that takes leadership from everyone. We have a responsibility to stand up for security. Leadership is action. This means we cannot be quiet complainers. Let's shatter the veil of silence and produce peace within our work. Let's propel safe conversations to the forefront and demand change. We hold the power. We are the key to unlocking better working environments. We must stand up and stand together. Our safety is non-negotiable. When everyone arrives at that place in their heart, where they know they deserve more and so do their co-workers, we discover camaraderie. And when there is solidarity, there is safety.

Everyone born in this world has human rights that must be protected by the law, including within our workplace. In 1948, the United Nations agreed upon thirty basic human rights that now make up the Universal Declaration of Human Rights.[2] Based on those initial thirty rights, every state, province, and country ratified their own labour laws that establish the rights for employees and employers. No matter where we are in the world though, we all have a right to be treated with dignity and respect, and have our welfare protected. There are ten rights within the UDHR that explicitly relate to how we have a right to a safe working environment. I became a certified human rights consultant to educate my sphere and shine a spotlight on the rights we already possess. We just need to know them to own them. If even just these ten rights were being upheld and cultivated in each place of work, we would never have mental and emotional safety hazards:

1. *All human beings are free and equal.* All human beings are born free and equal in dignity and rights. They are endowed with reason and conscience and should act towards one another in a spirit of unity.

2. *No discrimination.* Everyone is entitled to all the rights and freedoms, without distinction of any kind, such as race, colour, sex, language, religion, political or other opinion, national or social origin, property, birth, or other status. Furthermore, no distinction shall be made on the basis of the political, jurisdictional, or international status of the country or territory to which a person belongs.

3. *Right to life.* Everyone has the right to life, liberty, and security of person.

4. *No slavery.* No one shall be held in slavery or servitude; slavery and the slave trade shall be prohibited in all their forms.

5. *No torture and inhuman treatment.* No one shall be subjected to torture or to cruel, inhuman or degrading treatment or punishment.

6. *Right to privacy.* No one shall be subjected to arbitrary interference with his privacy, family, home, or correspondence, nor to attacks upon his honour and reputation. Everyone has the right to the protection of the law against such interference or attacks.

7. *Right to social security.* Everyone, as a member of society, has the right to social security and is entitled to realization, through national effort and international co-operation and in accordance with the organization and resources of each State, of the economic, social, and cultural rights indispensable for their dignity and the free development of their personality.

8. *Right to work.* Everyone has the right to work, to free choice of employment, to just and favourable conditions of work, and to protection against unemployment. Everyone, without any discrimination, has the right to equal pay for equal work. Everyone has the right to form and to join trade unions for the protection of his/her interests.

9. *Right to rest and holiday.* Everyone has the right to rest and leisure, including reasonable limitation of working hours and periodic holidays with pay.

10. *Right of social service.* Everyone has the right to a standard of living adequate for the health and well-being of themselves and of their family, including food, clothing, housing, and medical care and necessary social services, and the right to security in the event of unemployment, sickness, disability, widowhood, old age, or other lack of livelihood in circumstances beyond their control. Motherhood and childhood are entitled to special care and assistance. All children shall enjoy the same social protection.[3]

We stop violations by equipping the workforce with the knowledge of these rights and all the articles of the UDHR. Then it is the mandate of employers to educate their staff on their rights and uphold them. How many businesses have empowering mission statements on their websites yet suppress their staff's voice? Our workforce requires accountability from the top down. If our leaders don't pave a way for honest dialogues and safety, then the workplace is toxic. And when the bosses are the ones violating their employees' rights directly, it's more egregious. Like I shared before, most of my jobs violated the above human rights articles and made me feel unsafe. I couldn't articulate those feelings to myself, much less verbalize them to my employer.

I began one job excited and eager to learn and grow within the organization. I looked up to my boss as a mentor. I wanted to absorb all that she could pass down to me and I was willing to put the work in to climb the corporate ladder. I soon realized that I, a feisty, colourful, and out-of-the-box marketing girl, wasn't a good fit for this cookie cutter company. I was creating successful campaigns, reaching the community like never before, and making a big splash for our division, yet my boss continually picked apart my work and ideas. I was on contract and my main goal was to get hired on full-time, so I tried harder to win her approval. The more I did, the less impressed she was. She made comments about how underwhelming my work was. She pinned the office assistant and me against each other and we fought numerous times. By the grace of God, we somehow found a way to move through that together. I was set up to fail and then she berated me after the fact. Looking back, I think it was jealousy that this young girl did it a new way and got results. She couldn't verbalize that to herself, so she deflected the jealousy onto me in horrible ways.

This company prides themselves on safety to the extreme and yet I was gaslighted and tormented by my own boss. She dangled the carrot of a possible fulltime hire, yet plotted with upper management to get rid of me. At the end, I went to a manager in a different department and broke down. I told him

I obviously don't fit in, and he confirmed my worst fear. She had told the team she cannot work with me and is getting rid of me after a fundraising event concluded that I was lead on. I was devastated. It was a betrayal. I had never had a formal review. All the other bosses sang my praises and yet I was on the way out.

I once confided with a co-worker privately in her office how I felt like I was being used to have a successful event and then get dumped. I contemplated not putting in the effort just to stick it to them. But since that would only hurt the charity not my boss, I decided—after a good confidential cry in my friend's office—to still finish with character and integrity. Unfortunately, someone eavesdropped outside the closed door and heard my conversation. They didn't know it was me, but they knew with whom I spoke. My boss along with HR sat in a room with my co-worker and grilled her for information. They tried to coerce her to reveal the person who was ranting in her office. My friend didn't budge. She protected me at the cost of her own promotion. They bribed her for information. I am completely in awe of her loyalty to me. But I'm also sickened that a company would do such a despicable thing. This violates a list of labour laws.

As my boss was doing this behind the scenes, at my goodbye party she bought a hat for me from my favourite store. I was so confused and hurt that she could be so two-faced. My friend was livid over this woman's hypocrisy. On my last day, my phone line was cut off by 9 a.m. I was done. She didn't say good luck or goodbye. That whole experience broke me. Shame covered me for many years from what transpired there. Workplace trauma cripples you. She hijacked my confidence, safety, and sense of purpose. I went to therapy to heal all the mental and emotional wounds that my boss inflicted on me. Years later after doing a ton of personal work, I ran into her at a gas station. I said hi, she hugged me, and I felt no heart pain. I had healed. Sadly, my experience is all too familiar for people. This must stop and we must speak out. Mental safety is just as vital as the physical.

FLUX CAPACITOR

Ensuring our human rights are supported is everyone's responsibility, but those in positions of power or authority are held to a higher standard. We enter a sacred trust with the owners and management when we agree to work for a company. Bosses must maintain safety in all facets, not just the physical. When there is a secure umbrella over the energy of the company, the staff feel safe to communicate their ideas, issues, problems, and proposed solutions. I like to compare this to the mentality of a diplomat versus a dictator. A diplomatic boss listens first; a dictator tells. We think force is needed to lead and diplomacy is weak, but that mindset is flawed. People won't respect your force, they'll just fear you. To steer a company, one must inspire and lead not by command-and-control, but through influence, engagement, and cultivation of a safe and happy space. This creates respectful rapport. Some of the greatest leaders in our world mastered the diplomatic approach. Mahatma Gandhi, Nelson Mandela, Martin Luther King Jr., Ruth Bader Ginsburg, Abraham Lincoln, and Mother Teresa didn't rule with an iron fist, but with a soft heart towards humanity. Why are we not emulating their ways? We need connection and collaboration. Businesses need to incorporate the Flux Capacitor technology. In the popular movie franchise *Back to the Future,* a quirky scientist invents a time machine that runs on a flux capacitor. "In it, quantum 'tubes'

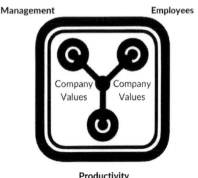

Productivity

of magnetic flux can move around a central capacitor by a process known as quantum tunnelling, where they overcome classically insurmountable obstacles."[4] When things are fluid, open, and reconciled with our values, there's sweet symmetry within the organization. We cannot fail when we are plugged into our core values and each other. One previous boss did use the flux capacitor mentality on us. Every person who worked for him grew into a better human because he inspired, influenced, and instilled confidence. It's a power source that will never run dry.

Once we have a leader committed to being a diplomat, we have open lines of communication with them. There is still onus on the employee though. We need to be secure in our identity and our voice to be able to verbalize our needs and wants in the workplace. The success of the flux capacitor requires the worker to set the tone and own their worth to establish the boundaries from the start. If you are not confident and lack communication skills, you risk an invasion of the boundary lines. I wish there were a communication training manual for employees on how to resolve conflict and on how to negotiate. Every workplace should encourage and nurture these skills. A better and more evolved employee creates an evolved company. If I had acquired these tools back when I encountered that horrible boss, I could have prevented an emotional breakdown. I wouldn't have lasted there either way, but a confident woman wouldn't have taken that abuse and would have voiced how unsafe that workplace really was. But I can't blame myself for what I didn't know then. Now I can do better because I know better.

The target of abuse is never to blame, but they can choose to find something from which to learn and grow. Now I make sure I set the proper tone from the start with every client I take on and with every contract I sign. I don't feel awkward for broaching a tough topic; I have taken my worth and my identity out of the equation and approach the issue with the aim of meeting in the middle. There doesn't have to be a winner and a loser in the conversation. We can both walk away as winners. When bosses want to see their staff win and when employees want to help their leaders triumph, that is success. Boundaries will automatically be respected when we aim to unearth a mutual beneficial outcome. This method prompts buy-in from all parties and fuels a community culture.

Just as it is vital for management to treat their employees with respect and kindness, it is also just as crucial for co-workers to treat one another with the same kind of respect. Harassment amongst co-workers is an epidemic. Colleague cattiness, competitiveness, and cruelty are the norms in any company even though most organizations promote anti-bullying and wear pink shirts every year. Just like our schools have taken on a kindness contradiction so have our workplaces. How can someone step forward and voice they feel unsafe when they have an anti-bullying program at work? How can adults be bullied? Shouldn't we be able to stand up for ourselves? This creates a level of shame and confusion and then ultimately a gag order on anyone wishing to speak out. The fear of being ostracized overrides the call to be brave. Everyone can relate to the following two confessions uttered to me:

> "This last year and a half I have been bullied by a couple of women and it has been the worst year of my life. I literally work, take the kids to school, and come home. It is so hard. I have seriously been contemplating moving."

> "Social isolation in group settings is brutal. I see it all the time in my work, cliques, etc. One minute you're in, then someone gets mad at you, and you're not asked to go on the lunchtime walk. Or you hear about how everyone went out for drinks after work and no one invited you, or everyone gets birthday cards except for you. It is a painful experience."

What is the solution?

> "I want to tell you a secret, a great secret that will see you through all the trials that life can offer. You must always remember this. Have courage and be kind." – Ella's Mother (Cinderella)[5]

I just heard this quote, and it sparked a profound realization. We cannot have kindness without courage. In a world filled with hurts and cruelty, when someone chooses kindness, they are incredibly brave. Let us tackle the problem by the root and teach employees to be reflective and understand that bullying behaviours come from internal hurts and insecurities. Let us encourage bravery to face those hurts and heal them. If we don't embody courage in the present moment, aren't we doomed to perpetuate the callous culture? The child bully in school becomes the tormenting co-worker. The cruel colleague today becomes the dictator boss tomorrow. Let's stop the spread of nastiness and promote collaboration, empowerment, and empathy.

Once we establish open communication lines from the heart of the company through to the management, a trickle-down effect results. Bridges from employers to employees are built and lead to cohesiveness from co-worker to co-worker. The result is an environmentally friendly workplace with free-flowing communications. This is symmetry at its finest, and it prevents burnout or shutdowns. The contribution from everyone ensures continual production. The feed can never be cut. What a welcome change from the current norms.

I want to promote the flux capacitor approach in every workplace. Could you imagine a charter of rights of communication interwoven with the flux capacitor method at the crux of every company? We would see a kinder and more courageous world. We would trigger an outbreak of confident people inspired to positively change the world. I was never assertive in my jobs. I was spiteful and jealous with my co-workers. My voice trembled when I wanted to pose a different approach with my superiors. I look back at that girl and want to take her by the hand and show her a better way. Not a path in which I dominate and crush others, but a route that guarantees safety for me and my comrades. This is the fuel for the future. The flux capacitor method will completely transform the workforce.

GENDER INEQUALITY

We will never see unified and friendly office spaces if we don't fix the gender bias. Unless we allow for women's super-identity to be restored, discrimination will rule as the kryptonite of equality, advancement, and peace. For the life of me I cannot understand why this is even an issue. Women are humans just like men. Women have rights under every law in North America, and yet here we are in the 21st century still fighting for equal rights. We make up half of the world's population. How have we not revolted against this? Probably because women have been pitted against each other since the dawn of time so we are unable to come together collectively and stop this violation of rights. But the fact that we have men who are married to women, who vow they love us and want to protect us, who have daughters they adore, yet don't stand up for gender equality mystifies me. This isn't a women's issue; it's a humanity one. No one should accept this as okay or normal.

Statistics show there is a pay gap in our work culture worldwide. If this section sounds angry, it's because I am infuriated to the core. The fact that we've known about this pay gap for many years but have done so little about it makes it exasperating. We acknowledge the imbalance and we do news stories on it and then we just move on. This is a travesty. According to the Canadian Women's Foundation, recent studies show women in Canada get 89 cents on the dollar compared to men.[6] They do a little better than the US, in which studies from the Economic Policy Institute say women get paid 22 percent less than men (78 cents on the dollar).[7] Since women's rights movements began, the numbers are improving but only at the rate of molasses flowing. Though we have made progress, if those numbers don't show equal pay, we are failing humankind. These stats are even worse for those of other ethnic backgrounds, minorities, or with disabilities. At this rate, it will take 267.6 years to close the economic gender pay gap worldwide.[8] This is unacceptable. In what world is that okay for our wives, daughters, granddaughters, and loved ones? We must speak up and act. Women's rights ARE human rights.

There is more to the gender bias conversation than just wages. Women's experiences are not unidimensional. Age, race, gender identity/expression, class, ethnicity, and sexual orientation also shape them. These experiences can increase a woman's vulnerability to enduring sexualized violence, harassment, and discrimination. This complex topic has infected many arms of the workforce. The stench of a deeply rooted attitude of male superiority permeates the walls of workplaces around the world. Sexualized violence is something every company speaks out against publicly, yet many don't enforce it. We like to think we have improved since the fifties, but we have simply gotten better at concealing the misogynistic behaviours around the office. I recently had the privilege of reading my friend Kirsten Anderson's book, *More Than Words: Turn #MeToo into #ISaidSomething.* She shares her personal story of sexual harassment, bullying, and retaliation and her pursuit of justice against the State of Iowa. Everyone needs to read this book. Anderson bravely exposes what is hiding in plain sight—male chauvinism.

Her accounts made me reflect on the moments I was a target of bias or sexism and of the sexual advances I so naturally shrugged off as annoyances women are supposed to put up with. There are some business leaders paving the way for women in a positive way but unfortunately, they are in the minority. Our world requires companies and employers to enforce gender equality. We need to eradicate sexualized violence of every kind. If women can't even feel safe to advocate for equal pay in the workplace without being punished or treated differently, how can they voice and champion their birthright to not experience sexualized violence? Every person on this planet needs to fight for equality and inclusivity. For as long as my daughter could potentially experience toxic masculinity, gender bias, or violence at work, I will continue this crusade.

Do you want to send your daughter or wife to work where her innocence and trust are endangered of being stripped by a co-worker or an authority figure? Where cowards desecrate her very dignity and honour? Where peer pressure and fear cripple anyone from standing up for what is right, decent, noble, and moral? If you and I don't take that stand against that every moment of every day, then we are participants in the problem. I challenge us to halt the hijacking of gender equality. We must take to task everyone who supports sexualized violence, even if their support is in the shadows. Another aspect of gender inequality that is barely spoken about is Women's Reproductive Health Rights. According to the Human Rights Commission of Canada, pregnancy in the workplace is a fundamental human rights issue of equality of opportunity; women should not suffer negative consequences in the workplace because they are pregnant.[9] The Canadian Human Rights Act (the Act) prohibits discrimination related to pregnancy, even if that woman is not yet pregnant but is trying or is suffering a pregnancy loss.[10] Businesses have a responsibility to educate their staff on how they plan to cultivate a culture of being advocates for women-friendly workplaces. They are accountable to create guidelines that support and uphold reproductive health rights and allow for mental health support, bereavement leave, or benefit help for their employees.

Women to this day fear informing their employers they are trying to conceive or are pregnant. If this is the case, women who miscarry are even less likely to say anything of the trauma they are experiencing. This isn't just a medical issue but also a mental health one, and therefore should be of interest to the company. We all got excited over New Zealand announcing they give leave when you have a miscarriage. Canada has the same laws but only if you experience loss within twenty weeks of the due date, leaving the miscarriages before twenty weeks in no man's land.[11] Yet since most miscarriages happen in the first trimester, the toll of grief and loss on parents is not being addressed. Though the law has good intentions, it falls short in truly supporting parents. Even if businesses comply with the faulty policies, employers must lead the conversation and advertise what reproductive health rights look like in that organization.

When I had my second miscarriage, I was at work. I bled baseball-sized clots and soaked through my pants. I made it to the staff bathroom and put my sweater over my waist and waited until my lunch break to go home and change. I didn't want my employer to know I was pregnant, and I didn't want to look weak and admit I was miscarrying. I had feared they would look at me differently and not even care. I quickly changed my blood-soaked clothes and returned to work within the hour. I was miscarrying and felt my only option was to deny my own body, trauma, pain, and femininity for a job. This is wrong on all levels. These are basic needs for mothers in the workplace. We must feel safe to be a woman in our work. It is essential our employers amend HR policies to reflect equal representation for fertility issues. It is the employer's responsibility to open the dialogue between management and staff on these matters and to ensure a safe environment for such discussions.

I became a certified human rights advocate with the US Institute of Diplomacy and Human Rights in 2020 and only then did I learn of Women's Reproductive Health Rights. I am committed to bringing awareness, education, compassion, and change to this issue through the Footprints: Infertility & Pregnancy Loss Support Initiative, my award-winning NGO. Our wombs need a voice in the workplace. Communication connects the womb in woman. *Fear, shame, anxiety over retaliation, judgment,* and *targeted* are a few words to describe what women experience daily due to gender bias. If women are paid less, experience sexualized violence, treated as subservient to men, muzzled, not represented, disrespected, not given equal opportunity, and undervalued at their place of work, they are casualties of major human rights violations. A culture of bias reigns from the top down in this world.

School gets out at 2:25 p.m. in British Columbia. I am blessed I work from home and can pick up my child in the middle of a workday but what about the average working parent? Do employers allow parents to leave early and take care of their children while still getting paid? Are there childcare options at work? It feels like the education system, governments, and employers are working against parents, especially working mothers. Because women are generally paid less, it is most likely the woman who must go part time or figure out alternative childcare. The lower wage usually means her job is seen as "less important" than the man's.

Another injustice is the pressure to return from maternity leave. Yes, Canada is much better than the US in this regard, but why are we pressuring mothers to return to work in a year or eighteen months? My baby wouldn't take a bottle, so I breastfed until she was over eighteen months. I wouldn't have been able to return to work before that time. The stress inflicted on baby and mother by putting them in this generalized timeline box is absurd. If there was a parenting process that made a father's dick and balls engorge and spring a leak at any moment, I guarantee employers would give allowances for men. Why is it so different for women? When we do return to the workforce and send out our resumes, we women are faced with explaining timeline gaps. How do we compete with others who didn't take five plus years off to raise children? How dare we say we deserve to be considered when we haven't been actively working in that field for years? And if by some miracle we get the desired job, we "should" feel lucky to even get the offer so we don't say anything about how little the pay is. I mean we can't expect to get paid the same as our male counterpart when they didn't take a five-year vacation from their careers, right? So many people say to me, "We don't have gender bias in our business. We provide equal opportunity." I challenge that. Because even if they do support women in the workforce, there's always room to improve. How many barriers did that mother overcome to get there? Raising awareness of the various adversities and hurdles women face to arrive at the same position as men might be a good first step to eliminating the bias.

Let's celebrate and reward motherhood. Can you imagine the difference in the office and in the home if the mother role was honoured? One common argument for men getting paid more is that they never took time off, so they shouldn't be punished. Another is that men are simply better at negotiating. Well, why is that? Why are men better negotiators? Could it be because women are never nurtured to push back and counter with salaries or opinions? We are just fortunate to be there, right? We aren't supposed to make waves or look entitled or ungrateful. If we do anything other than just say "thank you" and "yes," we are labelled as emotional, erratic, greedy, aggressive, selfish, or bitchy. To achieve a diverse and inclusive workplace, employers should not only provide equal wages for everyone, but also offer leadership training, encourage opportunities for growth, and ensure a realistic work/life balance. With these in place, women will be empowered to excel in their profession.

CULTURE OF KINDNESS

We need kindness to infiltrate our entire workforce. I came across the phrase "Culture of Kindness" while living in England when I met a British author and speaker, Nahla Summers. We were on a speaking tour, and she shared how one act of kindness from a stranger changed the course of her life. Her book entitled *Culture of Kindness* promotes kindness in the workplace and in our communities. I read her book, we became friends, and I've had her as a guest on my *Blaise the Trail* podcast. Every time we speak, I learn something new or encounter a fresh way to look at old concepts. The following points are from my podcast episode titled "A Culture of Kindness," with Summers as my guest.[12]

Every person who works for a boss, company, or organization craves kindness, and unfortunately most businesses are driving people away at an alarming rate. Just think about it. We all could expose a laundry list of problems at each company but if we really harnessed the spirit of kindness, we would solve many of those issues. Why is kindness so vital for the workplace? According to Summers, kindness makes up the umbrella of a value system that fashions people feeling seen, heard, and appreciated for who they are. If management embodied safety, gratitude, empathy, time, integrity, courage, connection, and being present with their staff, kindness would organically emerge as a core value within the workplace. If we could cease the unkindness cycle, we would see so many injustices including gender bias just melt away. Women wouldn't be paid differently because that would be cruel. We wouldn't have to fear sexualized violence or being treated poorly because those acts would be callous and shameful. People wouldn't be bullied, harassed, or taken advantage of because kindness is the opposite of those things. Kindness would drive workplace safety, which would allow for people to be honest and have the courage to speak the truth. Kindness is the connector. The Great Resignation is something that took place during the pandemic.[13] Corporations are losing people and money at a shocking rate. Workers aren't returning to jobs that treat them badly and there are staff shortages worldwide. Could simply shifting from a busy, cutthroat, and uncaring environment to a kind working atmosphere cause a Great Rebound instead?

Summers is working to change how we view the energy of kindness. It isn't fluffy; it's powerful. CEOs and business owners must be leaders in bringing the art of caring back into the work conversation, whether in the overall culture of how a business operates or in how we react to situations, adversity, or a crisis. Our reactions are just as important as our intentions. Most people would consider themselves kind, yet when are faced with an unpleasant person or circumstance, often respond in nasty ways. We require self-control, discipline, and reflection to be brave enough to seek out compassion. We need to embody empathy for our neighbour, whose part of the story we don't know. So often, we react from what we are seeing on the surface, but we must be willing to step back and try to understand the deeper factors at play before we issue our responses. Summers so eloquently encourages us to embed kindness in every part of our lives. We will be more emotionally intelligent because of it. And when we are guilty of leaning into a visceral hate reaction, let us own it, apologize, and walk forward in a kinder manner. I would love it if the next time someone faced workplace bias, they simply yet firmly stated to their superior that they are an unkind manager. Can you imagine the dialogue we could have if people just verbalized every unkind act and forced colleagues and managers to reflect on their own code of conduct? We would see a Great Rebound when workplaces celebrate every act of benevolence and refuse meanness. We all hold an immense power to alter the atmosphere in our office space. We just need to be gallant enough to choose compassion. Our peace and mental health depend on it. Gender equality demands it. Worker retention craves it. The human spirit deserves it.

As I consider my experiences in all my previous jobs up until now, compassion and camaraderie were often scarce or absent. There were times when I encountered kindness by bosses and coworkers, but sadly those experiences were eclipsed by the endless bullying, abuse, taunting, excluding, harassing, prejudice, competing, and chauvinism I suffered. I had some doozies of bosses that were cold-hearted jerks who robbed me of my dignity. I also experienced the cattiness of women as well. That was an even worse betrayal of humanity. My own sisterhood turning on me when they know the struggle women have already endured is akin to being kicked when I'm already down. Women are going into protection mode at work because they don't want to be the target of any mistreatment. To deflect it, they participate in the abuse against their own sex just to survive their workplace environment. If anyone reading this has ever been on the receiving end of another women's fear and hatred, I see you. I feel the silent pain you are going through. You are not alone. Women, stop hating on other women. There's a better way through this bias. If we could see the bigger picture and join in solidarity, we would have won half the battle. Kindness kills contention. Compassion fuels connection and growth.

There was an instance I felt immense kindness by my coworkers, and I want to celebrate it. When everything happened with my dad, I was working at a physiotherapy clinic. I was unable to work for a couple weeks while I navigated through what was happening with my family. I didn't have sick time or vacation time to use so I was on leave without pay. I honestly was so wrapped up in my circumstances that I wasn't really thinking about money until I had to pay my rent. Then one evening I had a call from one of the physiotherapists and she demonstrated pure compassion towards me. She cried with me and just expressed how much they support and stand by me. Then she ended the call with telling me all the physios and therapists had covered my desk over the previous two weeks so I would still get paid. After all these years, I remember that conversation like it was yesterday. It wasn't about the money, but about the gift of kindness bestowed on a hurting young woman. Their humanity humbles me to this day. If we could just harness that power, we would see a more empowered workforce.

Unfortunately, the world hasn't hopped on the kindness bandwagon. Those emotionally intelligent conversations aren't happening as often as we need. We just get rid of people rather than have honest, accommodating conversations. Fear rules and benevolence is the enemy. This kind of pattern drives stress and anxiety amongst the people. We need to look for what is at the root of the problem, not a scapegoat. To solve the cruelty crisis, we must have real discussions of vulnerability. Companies need to create morals to live by, not just a mission statement.

Summers is adamant it's vital for management to insist upon the kindness factor. Consideration for humanity must be present when having meetings and when holding people accountable. Summers claims the lack of kindness is a central issue that is ruining the workplaces. Fundamentality changing the culture in the workplace is key. It's not about funky staff rooms and mental health PR campaigns. Kindness breeds kindness. If we want our businesses to have brand identity, then having a human dignity identity should be at the core. We will never be able to connect employers to employees and staff to the consumer if we cannot communicate with respect and care. I want to see businesses thrive because they value integrity, honour, human decency, respect, and empathy. Productivity is a by-product of human kindness in the workplace. From there we will provoke the Great Rebound.

CHAPTER

8

VENUS

FEMALE DESIGN

The feminine and masculine forms are designed to co-exist with one another, not dominate each other. Yet we live in a society that still views the matriarch as supporting or subservient rather than a co-ruler. I am a feminist, but I think this label has become tainted and viewed as hostile when it ought to mean an advocate for gender equality. Feminism isn't about women taking over the world or dethroning men, it's about coregency. We need one another to complete the human design. We all possess unique abilities, strengths, and weaknesses. We cannot operate fully if we are heavy on masculine and light on the feminine, or vice versa. Humankind requires the balance of the two. It doesn't matter who we are, we all have unique and essential characteristics. These next two chapters explore learning about ourselves and others. This is more about connecting with humanity than gender. I am writing from a white, middle-class, heterosexual, cisgender, and educated perspective; but I promote inclusivity, diversity, empathy, belonging, and acceptance. The matriarch's purpose is to provide mother-like qualities to our ourselves, our spheres, relationships, communities, and the world. These traits include emotional intelligence, wise counsel, intuition, creativity, nurturing, childbearing, soft approach, cooperation, harmony, unwavering strength, resilience, resourcefulness, cleverness, ferociousness, innovation, joy, fluidness, wildness, and a resolute spirit.

To be a Captain Communicator one must recognize the potency of power the female design holds. Fear has kept the feminine force shackled for generations and generations, but to advance everyone, we need to join forces. Feminine and masculine characteristics are within us all. We can either relate to and learn from these traits in ourselves or seek understanding of others. To reconnect and have high-functioning comms systems, we must make friends with our feminine energy. How can men treat us as counterparts if we don't accept and celebrate our own superpower? Dr. Clarissa Pinkola Estés (author of *Women Who Run with the Wolves*) makes an interesting observation, "Within every woman there lives a powerful force filled with good instincts, passionate creativity, and ageless knowing. She is the Wild Woman who represents the instinctual nature of women. But she is an endangered species."[1] If we don't act now and change the course of the female design, this superpower will be extinct.

If we the sisterhood want freedom, equality, and to take our places on the throne, we must first understand what the essence of femininity is. Only then can we harness the power within. I went on an intense educational journey as I discovered the key to healing my outer body was exploring the innermost parts of myself. I dared to turn the mirror onto myself and learn. This led to my completing in-depth courses, training on the three brains, generating new neuropathways, healing traumas, and discovering strategies on self-reflection. Understanding how our emotions govern our organs taught me about trigger and trauma responses. This awareness aids in changing the direction of my life with healthy coping mechanisms and decoding tools. I am able to stop the internal attacks and bring peace and balance to my mind, soul, and body.

No, I don't have a degree in psychology, but what I do have is first-hand experience of pulling myself out from the pit of darkness and doing the gruelling self-work to be able to write this today. For the last seven years, I have been a sponge learning and absorbing why I act or react and think the way I do. I am discovering the root of my *dis-ease* so I can change the narrative with my communications system and be the best me. In the process, I hope to help heal humankind too.

The key to unlocking the influence and power of the matriarchal purpose is to understand how we operate. Let's break this down. The left side of our body represents the feminine energy and the right side, the masculine. Everyone has a variation of both within themselves. If you could split your body right down the middle and examine all the ailments your body experiences, on what side do you feel neck pain? If it's the left, it could mean you are resisting the feminine or if it's the right, you might be having issues with the masculine energy in your life. Rigidity is the kryptonite to femininity. We tend to hold tension in our jaws, necks, shoulders, wrists, hips, knees, and ankles, and the lack of flexibility in those areas becomes a litmus test for our rigidity. Women are called to be fertile. But not in the archaic sense that we are solely here to reproduce and be ornamental for men. Fertility isn't linear. To be a matriarch, we must master the art of birthing. And we can't birth things if we are stuck, inflexible, or rigid. We must go with the flow.

The feminine is fashioned to birth babies, business ideas, world solutions, peace, unity, vision, movement, strategies, expansion, giftings, talents, artistic expression, sweetness, and love. We need to embody what we were designed to be and stop trying to be something we are not. This is why we see so many people rejecting the feminine. It hasn't been safe to be the matriarch or womanly.

When we can learn to truly mother ourselves and the people around us, we will see an empowerment transformation. We must explore the power of the feminine—emotional intelligence. Author John Bradshaw explains that "E-motions are energy in motion. They are the energy that moves us—our human fuel."[2] If we don't express our emotions, the energy becomes repressed. Often our suppressed emotions manifest as a harmful energy rather than a healing processed one. Emotional energy drives us, as does all energy. To reject emotion is to disconnect from the fuel of life. The essence of womanhood is the birthplace of emotions. When we are connected to our feminine superpower, we intrinsically communicate a sweet exchange of intimacy through the ebb and flow of our own existence. In this zone of genius, our interactions automatically generate the perfect pitch of energy and emotion. The feminine is about *being*, not necessarily *doing*. Intention on feeling and being present with ourselves nourishes this space. But when we are imbalanced, armoured, and unhealed, our interactions become tainted with excessive doingness, bitterness, judgement, inadequacy, resentfulness, and disconnection. Our emotions are our ally, not our adversary. They are the life-giver of our systems. We are not hysterical women because we express emotions, we are tapping into the intricate part of our female design. The womb-man is the core of the ultimate power source, the standard of intense strength and brilliance where one can literally create life. It is safe to be in the womb space.

When we operate from that ease of authenticity, we take on all the attributes of a wild woman warrior. We possess power, fluidness, persistence, resilience, and resourcefulness. These become built-in tools to access as needed depending on whatever situation we are in. This is how we can be calm in the chaos, multi-task twenty things at one time, process and release emotions, feed our babes, heal, be the peacemaker and diplomat in conflict, mentor the next generation to be world changers, nurture, and morph into a courageous crusader. We need to break the stigmas surrounding feminism and inject buy-in for feminine empowerment. It is time to pick up the mantle of the matriarch.

It is a passion of mine to intensely study the behaviours of people and to discover where these behaviours all stem from. Since the dawn of time, a human's needs and how they behave haven't been that complex, but culture continues to complicate things and muddy the waters. The truth is everyone just wants to be loved, accepted, belong, seen, heard, and valued, and have a sense of purpose. And when those needs are unmet, we veer off into negative ways to compensate. I know this well. Because I had viruses in my systems and severed connections, I didn't know how to defrag and reboot. Years of believing the lies that I wasn't good enough led me to invalidate others instead of just validating myself. I got competitive and jealous.

This behaviour traces back to the ancient caveman mentality. Scarcity was real and there's something innate built into us to survive. When we feel like there's not enough protection, power, validation, or belongingness to go around, we see the feminine energy dip into those toxic coping patterns I mentioned. We get aggressive and possessive. Other women become our threat and then we tend to lash out at one another. I have done this and experienced this. I would ever so slyly talk about someone behind their back. I also participated in gossip and mean-girl mentality. I excluded women who triggered those feelings of insufficiency. To regain power, I also emasculated men. I took shots at them to bring them down to my level. This was the wrong approach. Mocking how little a man earns, his lack of education, his height, his manhood, or anything he does is emasculation. Being controlling and making all the decisions also deprives someone of their strength. This doesn't expose their shortcomings, it reveals ours.

There were also times I was on the receiving end of those backlashes of inadequacy. It cut deep. We should not be each other's enemy. We hold the power to shift the atmosphere if we just could realize how to be one another's assets not assassins. Still, to this day I am bombarded with others' hatred stemming from the feminine energy of feeling threatened. Sometimes it's what I say and sometimes it's just my very presence that can disturb the demons hiding inside. As funny as it sounds, I just needed practice on how to handle the assaults. I am much better at it now. It still hurts a bit, but I'm able to put my shield up and decode the interaction, own my triggers, untangle the exchange, and then commit to understand why this other person is attacking me with such ruthlessness. Most of the time I arrive at empathy: they haven't worked through their trigger yet and it's not my problem. This is a big step to healing the feminine divide. We are safe in one another. Stand down. We are far more powerful uniting than tearing each other apart and being the last woman standing. Let us put back the unity in the feminine community.

OPPRESSION

Another portal through which to examine the female design is looking at the oppression factor. In every culture, religion, and country, women battle gender bias. I don't believe any group starts off with that intention, but humans have distorted meanings and teachings to create a hierarchy over protecting equality. As a Christian, I will focus on my own faith and how this particular lens might contribute to the imbalance. Look at the story of Adam and Eve in the Bible—the beginning of man and woman. We hear discussions all the time asking the question "Who was at fault for original sin?" Was it Adam or was it Eve? It's the woman who gets the blame because she ate the forbidden fruit first and then gave it to Adam. People also say since Eve was created from Adam's rib men are superior to women. Why did God create man in the first place? According to the teachings of creation in Christianity, it was for connection with and companionship for God. But then he realized man also needed companionship and help on earth and so God took Adam's rib to create woman. Here's where things get distorted. In Hebrew rib doesn't mean one individual bone but translates to *side*, meaning half of Adam went to forming Eve.[3] They are two equal sides. They are partners, equal in God's eyes, designed to be each other's counterparts and to lead side by side.

Another interesting misinterpretation is that when the first sin took place, God asked Adam and Eve what happened. Their responses became the root of what's causing so many problems with gender inequality in Christianity. When God confronted Adam he replied, "The woman you put here with me—she gave me some fruit from the tree, and I ate it" (Genesis 3:12 NIV). Right then and there Adam blamed Eve. He didn't own it, shoulder the guilt, or say he was sorry. He blamed someone else. We tend to do that today; we justify our actions by blaming others. "They did it too." "It was their idea." We deflect to lessen our own accountability. Now pay attention to what Eve said. "The serpent deceived me, and I ate" (Genesis 3:13 NIV). There's a tone of shame in that response. The evil serpent successfully executed his assignment against women and men.

God wanted companionship and connection for men and women but that was broken. When one side blames and other side feels shame, there is lack of connection, trust, and intimacy. The connection is severed. Man lost respect from God and for himself and woman felt at fault and ashamed. Adam was supposed to protect Eve but instead he betrayed her. We see the same tendencies today. Men are seeking respect, position, and power and women carry intense shame, anger, bitterness, and persecution. This is just one observation from a Christian perspective, but groups all over the world mirror a power struggle between genders to this day.

Trauma is another contributor to the oppression of women. No matter where the root of persecution of women stems from, the cruelty against us has undoubtedly caused generations of trauma. When we have suffering, we have trauma responses. Pain affects everyone, but for this chapter I'm focusing on feminine experiences. Some biases that are widely associated with women say we are weak because we show emotion. We are hysterical when we cry, so we cannot be trusted in leadership positions. Our families are deteriorating because women are demanding to work instead of staying at home. We get paid less because we have taken time off to raise our families and therefore don't have the same experience or confidence to negotiate as our male counterparts. We mustn't dress provocatively or give off harlot signals so we don't entice men to make advances on us. Marital rape isn't a thing. If we get pregnant out of wedlock, it's our fault for seducing men and they are not culpable because "boys will be boys." Women are not as good as men.

Women's roles are to have babies, be maids, cook, and take a subservient role to their partners. We should be good little women and play nice because we are lucky to get this much. Good ladies don't say no; they are agreeable, sweet, and smile. This narrative traumatizes us and keeps us handcuffed to the cycle of discrimination and gender injustice. We react to the trauma and then we are criticized for our reactions. As society continues this cycle of oppression, we all become active participants in tormenting womankind. We have bred a culture of trauma responses across the board. Women now think we need to fight for power, and men feel threatened. If we really look at the base of everyone's insecurities today, men don't want to feel weak, and they do everything to ensure they haver power and control and are respected. If something or someone threatens that value system, they become the enemy. And women fight against the notion they are not worthy, equal, or loved and they have become bitter about it. Time and time again, instead of focusing on how to move forward together side by side, we have gotten wrapped up in the blame game. "I've done this much; you've only done that." "You're doing it wrong." "I can do it better."

Now men try harder to feel respected and keep blaming women and pushing them down to avoid being perceived as weak. They try to be the best man and fight other men to be considered strong, powerful, and the ultimate alpha. Women try to take men's power away and disarm them because they have never felt equal; by emasculating them, they try to bring men down to level the playing field. And when we women don't feel loved, we withhold respect. What a vicious cycle. Then women lash out at other women to deflect from admitting we don't feel worthy or enough. We nitpick at others when we are really nitpicking at ourselves. The toxic power struggle will continue until we as a collective stop it. We are all equal, we just need to believe that and begin owning that title. Once we truly embody equality from a heart-wisdom space, others will respond to our newfound energy. We need one another to make progress in life. Let us fight together instead of against each other. Everyone, stand tall. Raise your head and put your shoulders back. We are worthy. We are beautifully and wonderfully made.

Like I mentioned before, I was one of these women. I have experienced bias, cruelty, misogyny, abuse, unwanted sexual advances, sexualized violence, and was made to feel small. So, to find some power, I tried to depower men. This never worked though because it's not about one upping the other sex, it's about everyone discovering they are worthy and have a unique purpose on this earth. We must connect everyone and work towards a common goal.

When I began to fan the flames of my husband instead of blowing them out, I saw connection and power at their finest. Two flames make a stronger fire. I didn't lose authority by encouraging and supporting him; instead I empowered myself in the process. His dreams became my dreams and I saw a shift. My husband responded with the same commitment to champion me. We are stronger together. We fuel each other when we work together. We have found success because we decided to focus our energy on the challenges of life rather than engage in a fight against each other. We are teammates—a band of partners. I also started shifting my behaviour around my dad and other men. I don't need to overpower them. I don't need to feel defensive or unsafe. I stand in my power and worthiness, but I also give them room to be empowered as well.

It's been a remarkable journey to develop admiration for others while emerging from a healed mindset of equality. We still have a long way to go for social justice for women's rights, but the people I now encounter are not my adversaries. I make peace with the masculine. I join forces with my male counterparts. With this revelation, I step into a vortex of influence and authority. Connecting to the masculine and feminine within and then welcoming both in others is our superpower.

THE VOICE

Tapping into the power of the feminine voice is vital to becoming a communication champion. But first we need to dissect the voice of Venus. Verbal and non-verbal expressions are the foundation of communication and communication is the heartbeat of how the world functions. Most women excel in both. Effective communication is about active listening and eloquent language. Not only does the feminine voice have a sweet speech, but it also possesses the ability to detect feelings and body language with intuitive precision.

When someone uses feminine-style rhetoric, they use a voice and essence that attracts the listener to evaluate their personal views against what the speaker is saying. When a shared reality is found, understanding through identification transpires. This is so powerful because it encourages the listener to act with an empathy based on their own experiences. This is different than the masculine-style rhetoric in which motivation occurs through conveying authority or dominance. The masculine helps drive action but the feminine understands what drives people. The two methods are a dynamic power couple.

We all have masculine and feminine frequencies and can appreciate the qualities of both. And yet, the feminine voice has been discounted, shamed, and outright muzzled for generations. We must create safety and an urgency for women to connect themselves to their voices. An astounding force lies within the feminine voice; we just need to tap into it and unbridle it. I want to see a world in which women know how to use their words with the grace and power they possess by using the proper tone. Getting intimate with how we interpret signals and process the messages in our inner dialogue is key.

Our internal comms system drives our external ones. Healing oppression and trauma will flush out clogged lines and recalibrate us. Our brains can then regenerate new pathways to effectively transmit our words and body language. When we can commit to the path of being unmuzzled, we will solve the identity crisis in women. We carry the keys to breaking the chains of silence and shame. We are the gatekeepers of our own voices. We hold the power to change the tone of this world. By unleashing sweet sounds and wise vibrations, we will tune the pitch of this world with our words. We just need to embody the voice of Venus and rise up as a Captain Communicator for all womankind to connect humankind.

To harness the power we have with our voices, we must build confidence to speak. Our authority, influence, poise, and strength all come from standing in the safety and security of our unique dialects. To walk in that kind of self-assurance, one must practice. To learn is to try. To master is to never quit. Even when the feminine expression is considered weak, we must continue exercising our voices. Conditioning ourselves to communicate by capitalizing on our feminine intelligence will forge us into experts of expression. Women have the power to be creative, insightful, empathetic, innovative, constructive, graceful, spirited, captivating, and influential. Those qualities are anything but weak. Practicing self-assurance helps us shift the perception of these attributes and positions them under a new lens. Power can be brute strength or found in the undercurrent. We need both. Women are just as strong as men, but in a different way. Learning how to communicate by keeping boundaries while not hurting others will be crucial. Decoding the sent, delivered, and received signals and transmitting them with a sweet tone invites peace and offers space for advancement.

I had to practice using my powers for good and not for destruction. For so long I hid behind my career as a broadcaster. The mask of the mic gave me a platform for my voice, but off the air I didn't channel the voice of Venus. I held no boundaries. I allowed people to violate me with their words and when I responded out of trauma, my voice was venom rather than the anecdote. So, I made it my mission to get better at the exchange. Just because someone spues poison from their lips doesn't mean you have to drink from their cup.

But to get better, I had to practice being in conflict. I had to keep trying; I fell and got up and tried again. Each time I entered conflict, I tested another tactic. I almost never get it

100 percent right, but every time I get better at it. And what was birthed from this experience was a valiant voice. One that is confident and possesses convictions. A voice that is committed to healing and not hurting because communication has less to do with how a message is intended and more with how it's perceived. To be a Captain Communicator one must realize that intentional listening is the secret. The more I listen, the better I get at forming the right tone and words. And the more I stay in a space of being tuned in, the better transmitter I become. The frequencies are crystal clear.

To own a victorious voice, one must take responsibility for one's own triggers. I've spoken about the trigger in previous chapters, but this is also vital for the voice of Venus. If we don't tame the trigger, we allow it to control us. The triggers silence the feminine voice. It is our birthright as women to express ourselves, and we are the driver of how we use our language. When we can shift the perspective, regulate the reaction, and change the narrative, we subdue the trauma response. It is necessary for women to face their fear and their foe and not mask their triggers but instead co-exist with them. This is how we become champions of communication. We will never get rid of our triggers but by studying them, we take authority over them.

Get to know your body and mind. What happens to you physically when you enter the trauma trigger and you want to react and deflect with wounding words? Keep a mental list of how your body changes when you are in conflict. When you detect those visceral bodily alarm systems going off, decide to take control. This is where you put on the cape and rescue yourself. We have internal superpowers available to access when in trigger mode. The vagus nerve, one of the cranial nerves that connects the brain to the body and runs from the brain to the large intestine, is the foundation of this. The vagus nerve system neutralizes the fight or flight symptoms and sends our bodies into a relaxation state. It is linked to our vocal cords and our throat, and travels down both sides of the body. It plays a major part in how our bodies and brains function. If it is atrophied, we can't even do basic tasks. However, by stimulating it we can step out of the victim role and into hero mode. By doing deep belly breathing, humming, singing, or massaging our throats, we can engage the vagus nerve and dethrone the power struggle of the trauma response. Try the following steps the next time you are triggered.

Calm: breathe and release the strain in your body.

Detach: create space between you, your emotions, and the issue.

Centre & Ground: move your focus from your anger/pain to the center of your body and feel your feet on the ground.

Focus: choose a word that represents how you want to feel in this moment. Breathe in the word, be present in the moment and feel your body stand down. This creates a safe pathway to listen, hear, translate, process, and respond in an empowering state.

Though the world might devalue the feminine voice, it is imperative that we as women don't reject it. Instead, we must embrace it and contend for the freedom of our expression. When we create safety around the voice of Venus, we give ourselves permission to be powerful, clever, significant, and in sync with our feminine energy. We open a platform to channel our superpowers into solutions and harmony for humanity. We take back the controls and reassess what our words are worth. The value of our expression is more precious than gold. It is a treasure to stand in our truth and contribute to connections and construction of this world. We cannot advance without communication and women are designed to bring sovereignty with their sound. We need everyone to fight for the safety for our voices. Without security, we cannot fully own the platform. Each day we all must stand up and be warriors for our voices. We must protect the very riches that will calm the chaos, end wars, create peace, provoke healing, end barrenness, birth love, shatter barriers, and build bridges.

When we feel safe, we consent to embodying femininity in its purest form. This makes room for a mosaic of tones, dialects, styles, sounds, and accents. There is also potency with our silence. Wisdom to know when words aren't needed delivers ultimate power. Sometimes silent grace is mightier than our loud mouths. And when needed, our diverse voices, formed from the essence of the feminine, are safe to be expressed.

COLLABORATION

Teamwork is central to empowering women. We cannot progress without working together. We haven't seen an explosion of equality because women are pitted against each other and men feel threatened. Removing the energy of hostility and competition shifts the atmosphere. When we face forward and attack issues as a collective, we see change. We no longer engage sideways; instead we advance towards empowerment. Collaboration is key but it is not the goal. Rather, when people feel seen, heard, and valued, they automatically draw towards cooperation. The objectives for the Venus are to be valued and to value others. This will drive solidarity and activate expansion as a unit. I examined all the interactions I've had with my husband, friends, family, and co-workers, and every time I felt appreciated, I wanted to work with them. It goes back to the old proverb "You catch more flies with honey than with vinegar." Growth is achieved through motivating our world to come together in harmony, not through repelling one another and triggering conflict.

If women can pause and digest this concept before reacting, alliances would form. We ought to recognize that if our inner heart's desire is to be seen, heard, and valued, others are seeking the same considerations. But if everyone is different, how do we do this? Demonstrate compassion and willingness to understand. Acknowledge that you've heard their words and that this topic matters to them. Ask clarifying questions so you can confirm active listening. Be curious without judgement. Seek ways to support them. Accept that your role is often not to fix things (do), but to hold space (be). This makes room for cohesive collaborations.

Women moving together in unity hold immense power, but we also need to partner with others. We belong at every table. And if we are not invited or are deliberately excluded, we mustn't force our way in but use the strength of our sweet words to influence. This will change minds and hearts. It will incite invitations. Our communication is about connections. If we are disconnected from Venus and Mars, we are not effectively harnessing the portals of communication. When I approach ideas, projects, and initiatives with a humble energy and not ego, I organically get welcomed in. The old me was good at pushing through and taking someone else's seat, but there can be no security in that approach because someone eventually reciprocates that behaviour. Eventually, I shifted my approach. When I embodied respect for my colleagues, requests to sit at the table flowed my way. Nothing can be transformed without respect leading the way. Even if you are gathering with groups and individuals who have opposing views or agendas, conducting yourself with honour is key.

Charm the atmosphere by your disposition. You will move mountains with a noble reputation. We will be magnets for all consortiums. The Venus essence can create a seat at the head table without our saying a word. And when we do speak, our voices will be heard.

Once women master the art of being magnetizing, we need to make it safe for others to pursue partnerships with us. Since we have gotten the rap of wanting to dethrone the masculine, we must prove we are safe to work with. By upholding the goal of collaboration, we verify we aren't a threat or looking to dominate. When men feel safe with women, they will be receptive and responsive to our suggestions and solutions. We are stronger together. The complementary qualities of the masculine and feminine are the recipe for world peace. The right balance of both is paramount. When women come together in harmony and attract men to partner with us, we fuel the future. We no longer get stalled by endless bickering and fighting but move ahead with a mutual understanding that we can't win without one another. The more I aim to help people in my life feel valued, the more receptive they become. I don't seduce, manipulate, bully, or subdue them. Instead, I come from a place where my intentions are their goals as well, and their hearts are stirred to support me. Fight forwards as a collective, not as enemies. We are the answer when we continually cooperate. When the moving parts all work in tandem and do their unique job, we witness total triumph. Women, it is crucial for us to stand down that we may stand up righteously. The stance of Venus engulfed in our charming energy is our power.

To capture the spirit of Venus, we must allow the mothering trait to lead the way. Anyone can be a mother. Whether we physically give birth or not, we are here to create and nurture. We are Mothers of Purpose. When we sign a soul contract with that statement, we validate the design, function, and form of the feminine. For thirty-three years of my life, I didn't understand the meaning of my life or the purpose of it. This caused me to seek validation in my doingness and not in my very beingness. I didn't know I had a unique destiny, and after going through so many traumas, hardships, and setbacks, I believed the lie that my future equalled pain and barrenness. When I didn't mother myself, I couldn't foster meaningful relationships. The disconnect within me created barriers with others.

But when I realized that I control the narrative of my life and could make a choice to rise from the ashes, I produced a life-altering decision. I embodied the power of Venus. I took up the mantle of the mother and became confident in my calling. This healed the severed communication lines and brought the flow back into my life. My soul became injected with love, hope, peace, and passion. This renewable energy fueled my dreams. The more you walk in the purpose of your life and participate in creation, the more fertile and self-assured you become. A mother's mantle draws people in. The core of the feminine power is the ability to cultivate partnerships that stand the test of time. Alliances forged through the heart of a mother are committed to the cause. I attract powerful unions with the sweet scent of a mother. One that is nourishing, inspiring, supportive, pioneering, mighty, intuitive, and magnetic. Both the masculine and feminine seek to work with me instead of against me. I changed the course of my life, all because I transformed the meaning of mother. When we harness the strength of the mother in our collaborations, we build impenetrable bonds. From the womb, we birth the answer.

CHAPTER
9

MARS

MASCULINE DESIGN

What first comes to mind when you hear "masculine design"? Is the male aspect a friend or a foe in your narrative? We live within a patriarchal system, and many believe the only way to achieve gender justice is to dismantle the oppressive structure of patriarchy. I disagree. We need to redefine the essence of the patriarch and restore its purpose. True feminism isn't about taking over and abolishing the masculine. It's about equal distribution of power. We need the matriarch and patriarch to co-rule. But first we need to understand the original point of the patriarch. We as humans have distorted the intentions and cut the communication lines between the two planets. Mars is now a hostile environment rather than a safe one. Social systems have been corrupted with viruses that tip the scales of dominance and power. Instead of dying to ego and drawing on the power of unity between the masculine and feminine, we embody the weakness of the patriarchy system rather than its strengths. When we have too much Mars and not enough Venus, we often become over-controlling as a strategy to gain authority. This can also manifest as excessive competitiveness, arrogance, aggression, greed, and judgmental viewpoints.

With an over-charged masculine energy, we can fill life with constant activity, which often results in workaholism, obsession with physical fitness, or the driving pursuit of unrealistic goals. When Mars is spinning out of control, we need to capitalize on the fluidness of the feminine to counterbalance the intensity of the masculine, and thus bring Mars back to optimal function. The male design is neither bad nor superior. It is essential to life—in balance with the feminine. In this state of equilibrium, we tap into true inner strength and authentic power while moving away from the unhealthy desire to gain power over one another. The balanced patriarch is fatherly and knows that a combination of patriarchal and matriarchal wisdom is needed in our governing structures. He knows that society will not flourish until there is an alchemy between the masculine and the feminine. When either masculinity or femininity are exaggerated, disorder and *dis-ease* result. Like I discussed before, I am referring to human behaviour and energies rather than gender. This section is an opportunity to reflect on our own tendencies and appreciate how other people operate.

The masculine within holds the seat of power and when operating in its zone of genius, our whole system becomes energized which in turn fires up our personal willpower, drive, self-esteem, and sense of purpose. This energy also fuels the health of our digestive system and muscles, as well as the pancreas, responsible for insulin production. The inner warrior is the hero or heroine who operates instinctively through gut intuition. We need effective communication from Mars to trust our gut and make wise choices. This is how we return to the original male design and walk in the wisdom of the warrior.

The traits of the masculine and feminine are very different from each other but both are crucial to the balance within our bodies and within our world. In the body, the right side harnesses our male energy (giving), while the left side channels our feminine energy (receiving). The Venus is empowered by being and the Mars thrives on doing. The way we express masculine or feminine energy (through physical, emotional, mental, and behavioral patterns) is shaped by our genetics, upbringing, environment, or is established in reaction to trauma.

Ailments present in the right side of the body indicate negative patterns associated with our masculine energy. An unbalanced right side can manifest as over-giving, people-pleasing, and relinquishing personal values and boundaries. Feelings of weariness, frustration, resentment, anger, and a lack of energy can surface. On the flip side, this imbalance can also manifest as being incapable of giving because the fear of lack or loss has forced toxic stagnation and selfishness. To release the blockage with the masculine and activate free-flowing movement again, we must take responsibility for our own life. Everyone is the keeper of their mind, body, and soul. This guardianship helps us better understand ourselves and others so we can communicate with ease. So, to balance the Mars within, we must consciously take ownership and walk in action mode. We mustn't blame others or our circumstances. Since the masculine is susceptible to excessive dominance, it needs to keep sight of its unique purpose, ambitions, and goals and take the right steps forward to achieve them. Think of staying in your lane. Being reliable is key, as is creating good boundaries. The empowered masculine discovers enjoyment and enthusiasm and practices self-discipline. The focus shifts to being a contributor instead of a conqueror.

When we foster the Mars traits in ourselves and support them with our counterparts, we will see these positive and balanced attributes shine. This will also reinforce personal power, risk-taking, assertiveness, confidence, objectivity, critical and logical thinking, and strength of spirit. When we encourage the development of these characteristics, we build pathways of connection between Mars and Venus where they both can give and receive. As I learned more about myself and began the reconnection process within my inner world, I was also committed to appreciating how the masculine makes up my outer world.

Since I was experiencing so many issues with the masculine energy, I set out to peel back layers of various narratives or preconceived judgements and just get curious about men. This thirst to enter a shared reality with the masculine was the foundation of my newfound admiration for Mars. What I learned was mind-blowing. Mars isn't shallow or one-dimensional. The masculine is complex with many interesting layers. The more information I acquired, the more I admired the male form. Over time men became safe for me.

It was all because of Alison Armstrong. She has made it her life's work to uncover the mysteries of men and women and to educate the world on her findings. Every book and course of hers led me down a path of insight and awareness. She studied the male form at every age and provides an outline of the various stages of growth men have. Once we can identify the chapter we are on or where the people in our lives are at, we can better comprehend needs and values. We learn how to better approach our men to achieve the best communication outcomes. Though I'm speaking about the masculine here, we all need understanding, appreciation, and connection.

Armstrong breaks down the various stages of manhood into seven phases.[1] Ages one to twelve is the Page stage. This is when boys are challenging themselves, taking risks with bold moves, discovering, and being a hero. Next is the Knight period. From ages twelve to thirty-two, the behaviour shifts to competition, adventure-seeking, and having fun. Males entering their thirties move to the Early Prince stage which spurs a desire to envision their future Kingdom. The Mid Prince era is from thirty to forty-five. This is the building age where men build their Kingdom. They are nose to ground and solely focused on working and providing. The Late Prince stage is from forty to forty-five where the emphasis isn't exclusively about work. They make room for other things on which to put their energy and attention. During this time men can also land in a dark phase which we call the mid-life crisis. They begin to question who they are and what their purpose is. They require space to reconcile their needs and wants. This is a vital time for his partner to become his champion and for the people in his life to support him. The final phase is forty-five to fifty plus and is called the King stage. This is where he knows who he is because he chooses who he is. Some Kings evolve to the Elder stage in which they focus on giving back. When I looked at my husband and even my dad through this lens, I found myself full of admiration, empathy, and mercy for them instead of distain and resentment. When we understand the male form better, we love them for where and who they are in the current stage they are in.

We know the strengths the masculine possess. We also know we can't be over or under with harnessing this power. The best way to balance ourselves is to be acquainted with our strengths and weaknesses. That's the beauty of the feminine and masculine equation. We are designed to stabilize each other's shortcomings. The alpha/ego energy is the weakness of Mars. Too much masculine can lead to an authoritarian nature and war, but when paired with the feminine powers of diplomacy, we find unity, peace, and progression. But too much feminine energy can lead to indecisiveness and stagnation. One isn't better than the other. We need both to complete the picture.

Collaboration and regard for the unique planets are key. It's just like cooking. We can't have too much acid or have things too sweet. We cut the overpowering flavour with counteractive ingredients to establish balance and a pleasant taste. Mastering the balance of the feminine and masculine is an art. It is also a conscious choice. Everyone must decide daily to make room for one another and to be willing to work together. Only then can we see our patriarchal society partner with the matriarchal one. That's a world I want to fight for and live in. Mars and Venus moving in tandem with one another. The masculine protecting, defending, and providing, while the feminine is birthing, nurturing, and creating. This is the recipe for free-flowing communication and balanced transmissions.

OPERATION MANUAL

My vision for this chapter is to give the reader an in-depth understanding of how the male form operates. With crossed lines and miscommunication occurring everywhere, the only way to reconnect is to enter a shared reality with others. We do this by getting to know how we all function, what our tendencies and values are, and what makes us feel seen, heard, and loved. I enjoy drawing on others' expertise and perspectives to understand a broader scope of diverse topics. So, I sat down with my close friend who studied under Alison Armstrong, and we had a great discussion of how to create a guide in decoding the masculine.

Known as the Connection Specialist, Vanessa Lusignan began her quest to understand the hidden language of men because of her own issues with the masculine in her relationships and in the workplace. She discovered that no matter who we are trying to communicate with, approaching things with a partnership mindset yields results. Lusignan wanted to be a better partner, and by dissecting the energy she was presenting in exchanges, she found ways to invite mutual, safe energy from men. Women go through similar stages of development as men, but Lusignan shares that the intensity of these stages for men is much stronger. Can you imagine how much better our experiences would be if we approached our signals with a joint commitment to understand and appreciate where we each are coming from? When the feminine chooses to identify with the masculine, we cause connection. Lusignan challenges us to explore Mars. Discover what is most important to the people in your life by seeking what drives them, what motivates them, and where they spend their energy. This allows for a better capacity for patience and support. Instead of feeling hurt when a guy spends more time with his friends than us, we could recognize what stage he is in and not take it personally. This is likely the Knight phase and is vital for a man's development. So instead of isolating him from his wolf pack, women could occasionally invite themselves into the friends' circle and still support their partner's need for brotherhood. Opportunities for bonding time without our partners is healthy too. We can still have connection and closeness while making room for male socializing. This is a great tool to use when single and seeking a mate. When we can honour what stage people are in rather than try to change them or speed up their growth rate, we create positive pathways instead of division.

Another crucial point in the manual is to grasp men are simple. Lusignan explains men continually reinforce this statement, but women refuse to believe it because we are complex. Men mean what they say. Women tend to question a man's yes or no and inject extra emotion or possibilities because that's how the feminine operates. But men are very direct in their responses. To better understand men, we need to believe them at face value. As women, we tend to question a man's simple response because we ourselves say yes to various things that we might not have the energy for, or we feel guilty saying no. Men cannot possibly mean what they say because we don't. The masculine is also single-focused, while the feminine can be seen as a multi-tasker. When a man states his needs, it is clear-cut because he's not bringing in other emotions, scenarios, or desires. Women tend to contemplate ten other factors that could play into our responses. Single-focused isn't inefficient, lazy, or inferior to the multi-tasker; it's just different. We all have our own strengths. When the masculine can't give us attention when they are working, watching sports, texting, or sending an email, it's not because they're choosing to ignore us. They are designed to only focus on one thing at a time. I used to get so hurt when my husband wouldn't look at me when I was talking to him if he was surfing on his phone. My inner voice was resentful because I know I can do both. Now I challenge myself to wait for him to complete his task that I may then have his undivided attention. Mars gives us the playbook, but Venus must be willing to follow it. If we don't, we both end up with unmet needs and frustration and ultimately disconnection.

Next in the manual is debunking a misconception: because men are simple, they aren't very deep. Lusignan says this misguided belief occurs because women don't often give men the space or time needed to respond in a deeper way. Mars needs time and space to open up. Venus may ask a question of their partner or male counterpart and when no immediate response is given, she peppers Mars with more questions. This results in surface-level answers or a complete lack of response simply because men aren't given room to formulate a richer reply. I was guilty of this. I realized I asked a ton of questions but never got any answers from my spouse. So, I experimented with my approach. I posed a question and then paused. Women, we must wait. Men need time to process the question or information and then the space to articulate a profound response. If we get impatient and fire back with a reworded question, men have to abandon their first process and then start all over again. To women, it looks like they are ignoring us or not valuing our thoughts. This isn't the case. They are trying to come up with a worthy answer. But women get frustrated and then offer another variation of the query and by this time, men's brains are so overloaded and confused they just give up. When I chose to ask and then wait, I couldn't believe the outcome. It felt like an eternity to sit in silence but once I gave my husband the time and space to reply, I received the most insightful answers. This was a game-changer for our relationship.

Safety is key for everyone. Lusignan reveals that if men aren't opening up on a deeper level, it's often because they don't feel safe. So instead of asking "Why won't you talk to me?" we should rephrase the question as "What is making you feel unsafe with me?" A major contributing factor to the "unsafe space" mentality is when women are out with their pals, they tend to share all their grievances about their partners. Men won't open up if everything they do or say is scrutinized in the so-called "hen parties." There needs to be an NDA with certain topics to protect the well-being of the relationship. How can our partners feel safe if we betray their trust when we go out with our friends? Women share to connect with other women's stories, but it comes at the cost of our own relationship. Our desire to connect creates a disconnect with our partners. If we continually bash men, we feed the narrative that men are lazy, selfish jerks. We cannot operate in harmony from this place. Create a secure communication bubble by giving him a safe space and honouring an NDA. This will open a world of deeper interactions.

Safety in a relationship is a two-way street, but it doesn't have to be complicated. I like following manuals and formulas because they provide step-by-step guides to arrive at the desired outcome. Of course, every relationship is different, but if we could follow a general equation, we would feel protected and have room for authentic expression. It's like d=rt (distance=rate times time). We will go the distance with our partners when we allow space for the unique rate of our communication to be mixed with the time it takes to get there. With that recipe, we can turn arguments into discussions instead of blowouts and breakdowns. Articulating our emotions in a safe place is paramount for both partners. We can protect truthfulness and honesty when incorporating grace. Just like any formula, it takes trial and error to discover. Over time, we learn how to partner and communicate with one another when we take ownership for ourselves and ownership for the other person's feelings as well. Lusignan emphasizes developing discipline and self-control over our triggers. We tend to match the other person's energy in conversations. Don't match the negative energy, but help them redirect their emotions and give them space to decompress. Be an anchor rather than the fuel.

The last step in the operation manual is also another anchor tool. Lusignan describes this tool as the giving of time and space to allow someone to transition from one place or activity to another. Men require this changeover to have the capacity to fully be present and available for us. For instance, when a man comes home from work, they need roughly a twenty-minute hiatus to move from work life to family life. Often women see their partner walk through the door and they immediately hand over the kids, give a data dump of what happened in their day, and then say dinner is ready. Women do this because they want to connect and get a break from their day. I know I'm going to ruffle a few feathers with this but it's true. I was triggered by this point as well. Why does he get a break when I don't? Well, do you want 30 percent of your partner immediately or 90 percent after just twenty minutes? Try this approach and see the results for yourself.

I gave my husband his transition time when he walked in the door, and I was shocked by what transpired. The ritual of him changing out of his work clothes is part of the process of moving from work stress to family time. He pours himself a glass of wine and watches tv or uses his phone. It's not like he's not there at all; we chit-chat and he sits with our daughter, but nothing is expected from him until that transition time is up. Then he is completely plugged into our family. I used to have dinner ready the moment he arrived home, but now I push it back half an hour and I see a happier man because he got his time. Then when he's happy, he has more energy to give, and I benefit. My needs get met because my man can mentally, physically, and emotionally meet them. If we withhold the transition time out of spite, we are actively withdrawing from the relationship. Why deny our partners that time when we know it provides them with something they need? Lusignan affirms that we will receive back what we put into the partnership. If women pull away, the men will also pull away and disconnection occurs. Someone must take the first step. This invites the other person to draw in and create the desired connection. It all boils down to the choice of valuing connection over ego. Give space and time, and receive attentiveness in return. Can you spot these behaviours in yourself or your mate? This isn't about classifying gender; instead it's about curiosity, reflection, and awareness of how we all function.

THE BRIDGE

Even though we talked about the main points of the operation manual in the above section, this entire chapter really provides us a great map to navigate to a connection with Mars. Part of this process is about being the bridge rather than participating in a tug-of-war. We must start looking at our interactions from the perspective of teammates rather than adversaries. Too often we have a mindset that it's a power struggle, and both sides end up doing or saying things that hurt the team. Lusignan stresses that women need to resist the urge to emasculate. Venus instinctively feels the power balance is uneven and so we emasculate to create safety. But cutting the masculine down just to build the feminine up is fighting dirty. We must get to the bottom of why women do this. Where is the lack of safety coming from? Lusignan prompts women to ask the question, "How can I heal that?" The sooner women can create safety in their nervous systems, the sooner they can move into calm communication with men rather than remain in trigger-emasculation mode.

Often, we view conversation in the wrong light. We enter a dialogue as if it's a battle of the wits. We spar and try to one up each other. This causes disconnection. When we shift the perspective to playing a sport, we can view the other person as our teammate. Think about how we talk to our fellow team members. We build them up. We become each other's cheerleaders. So why don't we do that in conversations? There, we attack rather than uplift. Be the bridge by elevating and inspiring the other. People respond to motivation and inspiration far better than criticism and put-downs. The bridge is the only way to effectively send and receive messages. The bridge fuels the tank. The bridge creates safety and the inclination to draw closer.

Infidelity is a big indicator in relationships that someone feels like there is no bridge. Yes, the person that is being unfaithful must take accountability for their actions, but we must explore the why. Why did they feel the need to draw close to someone else? Where is the lack of safety and opportunity to connect with their own partner? What needs to happen to begin the bridge-building again? Typically, when people cheat it's because they are getting something from the affair that they are lacking in their own relationship. They receive adoration, admiration, and appreciation and they like that feeling. When women emasculate their partners, it weakens the bridge. I'm not saying it's the woman's fault when a man cheats, but it's a way of understanding the needs of our partners and how we can better meet those needs.

When we love people, we want to make them happy. So why would we refuse the very thing that fills them with love?

Women, we will see such a strengthening in our partnerships when we issue the invitation. This creates security and room for our partners to move towards us. It is our commitment to the bridge that will ensure commitment to us.

As I've pointed out before, men value respect as that's what makes them feel loved, and women value the feeling of being cherished and adored. Often instead of building a bridge with actions that support the construction of this kind of love, we withhold the very thing the other person desires. We think because we aren't getting our needs met, this means we must protect our love and not give it freely to our mate. When women feel a lack of love from their partner, they hold respect ransom and when men feel disrespected, they withhold their love. This vicious cycle becomes a toxic pattern rather than a well-oiled machine love match. What does respect look like for each person? What does love look like for you? Everyone will have a slightly different answer so it's our responsibility in a relationship to ask those questions and truly listen to how love is defined. When we emasculate men and refuse to give time and space, we are disrespecting them. This behaviour creates barricades and resentment instead of connection and intimacy. Women use emasculation as a weapon of choice in conversations. I was a pro at it. We have become so accustomed to doing it, we don't even notice when we geld the other. We are master emasculators instead of motivators.

There was a moment in my twenties when I was at a house party, and we wanted a bonfire. There was a pile of wood, but all these big burley guys had no idea what to do. They all were joking and asking where the gasoline was. Since I was a farm girl and building fires was a family rite of passage with my dad, I volunteered to assist the men. It's interesting how a lot of my emasculation stories stem from situations with fire. I think it's because creating fire means provision and power. So, if I made a fire better than a man, I was more powerful. As men gathered around me, I used the teepee method and then built a log cabin while growing the little flames into a huge inferno. My talent became a dagger though. Instead of just being a gracious contributor to my male counterparts, I made fun of all the guys there. I teased and shamed them that a little girl outshone them. As I reflect on my actions twenty years later, I am embarrassed. In that moment, I emasculated men to elevate myself. I wish I could tell that girl to stop, that emasculation only highlights our own insecurities. I didn't think men were safe back then. I didn't believe I was equal or had any power, so I emotionally castrated the men there that night. Now I do better because I know better. I choose to build up rather than tear down. I become the bridge.

Another key factor in the bridge process is supporting our partner's needs. Lusignan explains that when women uplift and show appreciation, we automatically foster pathways of connection with the men in our lives. Supporting their needs is a bridge. This makes them feel respected, heard, and productive in the relationship. We often associate feeling supported as a Venus thing but it's for both. This also goes back to our individual love languages and what support looks like for each person within a relationship. These tips are for everyone in any dynamic.

Support to me looks very different than what it does to my husband. It also ties in with expectations. Silent expectations of people, situations, and outcomes are kryptonite in any relationship and lead to unmet needs. It's okay to have a wish or vision of how something should look like, but we must ensure we verbalize this to our partner. No one is a mind reader. Having this dialogue is crucial to the bridge building. If we bypass the expectation conversation, we set each other up for disappointment, frustration, and breakdowns.

I experienced this on a recent vacation with my husband. The main point of the trip was to give him a break from a grueling time at work. We considered him getting away on his own to unplug and recharge, but we ultimately decided on a family trip. This holiday was mainly for him but our whole family had been through a lot, so this was a good opportunity for all of us to rest and recuperate. A few days into the vacation, I noticed my husband was absent all day. Instead of sitting down with him and going over needs and expectations, I went right into pissed-off mode. Rejection is a sore spot for me so when I feel like someone is distancing themselves from me, I get triggered. We ended up having a disagreement and I was upset because he wasn't meeting my expectation of the family holiday I had envisioned. And he shared how he thought this trip was for him. We sat there and realized neither had clearly articulated what our desires looked like for the vacation. My ideals clouded his needs. So, I shifted the energy of the trip and supported his need to have space to completely disconnect and have no responsibility or expectation of him. This resulted in him drawing closer to me and our family. Out the expectations. Don't keep them hidden. And ensure you have realistic ones as well.

In a mutually respectful and healthy relationship, both parties contribute by putting in equal effort. They trust their partner. Human behaviour shows us that the moment we feel unsafe or rejected, we pull back and hoard our love, respect, and effort—but we need to do the opposite. We must turn towards the other and extend our arms rather than draw the bridge up. The decision to champion my husband, even when I didn't feel like doing so, changed the trajectory of our marriage. I gave him space to come into his own and I morphed into a cheerleader instead of his criticizer. I also committed to chasing my passions. This lit a spark inside me which not only motivated me but also inspired me to encourage my partner. The more I advocated for Robb's aspirations, the more he fanned my flames. We put in 100 percent for one another. It's not about his goals versus my visions, but rather it's about our dreams as a collective. No one has to keep score when we are fully contributing to each other. I don't feel a lack of support but when I show up for him, he organically shows up for me. We work in tandem together. And when occasionally we are triggered or feel unsupported, we know it's coming from an emotional, mental, or physical depletion. With awareness, we approach the situation with extra compassion. We reinforce one another where the bridge has been weakened, and together, we protect the path of partnership.

NOW YOU'RE SPEAKING MY LANGUAGE

By approaching communication with respect and curiosity, the feminine and masculine begin to speak the same language. Though Venus and Mars are completely different planets with their own dialects, they can translate and understand one another through a joint commitment to do so. When they position themselves towards each other, they enter a portal with a unique gravitational pull that draws the two planets together and they can speak in sync. This special place allows for setting up healthy boundaries and honouring them. Men are fixers and protectors. They are always listening for the point or the problem so they can offer a solution. When the feminine approaches a dialogue, she can use this knowledge to effectively design her queries, comments, and discussions. When she knows how others operate, she can take a shortcut to the conclusion.

Learning how men process information helps us present better questions. Lusignan reaffirms that understanding where men spend their time, money, and energy is critical to deciphering what's important to them. They may not be as verbal as us, but their cues are powerful. Just as women want to feel valued, men also have a desire to be appreciated, whether it's receiving general gratefulness for being a partner or thanks for those little chores around the house. Women expect that to co-exist peacefully in a home, we all have a list of chores to accomplish. Women multi-task and take on many responsibilities without recognition or the need to be thanked for every little thing. Men require validation that they contributed and provided.

Lusignan provides a tip. When someone says, "Look what I did with the dishes, the lawn, or the laundry," they are seeking appreciation. It's very direct and we mustn't shoot it down and ignore the chance to value them. Say thank you. If we deny them that and make a comment of how we do that all the time with little recognition, we openly emasculate them. This disconnects the communication pathway. We all benefit with acknowledgment and appreciation for our contributions to the relationship.

Mutual respect is the language of love. When both planets commit to respect, this sets both transmitters up for success. What good is it if I am an awesome speaker but a horrible listener? How can I call myself a good communicator if I don't make an effort to present the information in the best way for the other person to receive it? We can all agree that women talk more than men, but is that trait because women give no room for men to communicate? Lusignan advises women to support silent space. We fill voids with endless words, but we must get comfortable with the unspoken moments. I was guilty of this. I hated the quiet gaps, so I just kept rambling on. I never made room for a pause so my partner could formulate a thought or comment. The stories I told myself were "Oh he's just quiet," or "He never talks to me." I am so thankful for the wisdom of Vanessa Lusignan. She helped me position interactions with my husband in a more positive way. Now, I sit in the silence. I bask in it. And sometimes it's just quiet and not much is said and other times I am pleasantly surprised at the deep conversations my husband initiates.

Silence is uncomfortable especially if we haven't learned how to calm our minds or thoughts. The hush seems to shine a light on the hundreds of rapid thoughts we have bouncing around in our heads. So, to distract from the mess in our minds, we create noise. It's a channel to transfer all the opinions, judgments, and clutter from ourselves to our partner, as if we view them as a garbage collector. Sometimes we do need to data dump but as I said before, we must alert them that we need them to be our bucket holder. But to have a shared respect, we must do the same for the men and be their bucket by offering silence. They may only fill a portion of the bucket or make a few comments, and that's okay. We communicate through the act of giving and receiving time and space. Stop the noise and see what surfaces.

How do you position your tone in conversations? In moments of conflict is there a level of shame or blame with your words? This is more difficult to avoid than you may think. During various workshops, I was challenged to communicate my frustrations without shaming or blaming. I had to take time to formulate my phrases in an elegant way rather than just wrap them up in accusations. To speak the same language as Mars, it is necessary to express ourselves eloquently. It's truly an art. In creating an inviting space instead of a hostile one, we offer a remarkable gift to the masculine, in which they can receive information in a place of peace. Every conversation is a chance to channel all our wisdom, to access the tools we have collected, and to begin an effective exchange.

Each partnership needs to discover what methods work for them, but role-playing and reversed monologues are helpful to many. It allows for the other person to see how they're perceived and what their partner needs in the communication circle. Lusignan reveals the reversed monologues have aided in her relationship and have added a fun and playful way to express needs. Sometimes we get so busy or caught up in our own mental mess that we forget or completely negate what the other side is seeking from the encounter. Instead of reacting and initiating the fight factor, try the reverse monologue method. This takes the guess work out of the equation since you literally tell the other person what exactly you need to hear and feel. The more we incorporate such techniques in our transmissions, the more fluent we become in each other's languages. To achieve free-flowing communication with Mars, we must commit to collaboration NOT competition. In effective communication, we avoid one-upping each other with our comments and focus on having an effective interaction. When we are aligned, we nurture the masculine to become Fathers of Destiny and own their protector role with pride. Do we want to participate in the give-and-take, or do we want to win? We have a choice in every discussion.

I have seen my husband blossom in his purpose because I mothered that part in him. I make a conscious effort to believe in him and it's awe-inspiring to witness the transformation of our conversations. I am committed to shifting the definition of patriarchy and to eliminating its often-negative connotation. Patriarchy is about partnership. When we honour the other side, we shape trust and establish loyalty. These elements strengthen the men in our sphere. When they can trust the Venus with their signals, they're driven to produce results and provide for the people they love. A man's identity is attached to his purpose, career, and ability to produce results. When men are given the time and space to thrive in their identity, they are able to meet us in that extraordinary collaboration space.

To every man I've encountered in my past life, I am deeply sorry for how I spoke. This was never about you but about me confronting my belief system around the masculine. It took trial and error, but I have healed those patriarchal wounds and you were all part of the healing process. Thank you for taking the hit so I could restore pathways to the masculine. To my husband, you proved to me men are loyal, trustworthy, and safe. You stayed even when I gave you many opportunities to quit and leave me. Words cannot express how grateful I am. You never gave up on me; now we speak the same language and are more powerful than ever, working together and striving together.

There's one more man I would like to mention who played an integral part in my life. Rob Scheller was a mentor and one of the first people to demonstrate to me that men could be safe. He coached me in fastball and trained me to improve my craft and character on and off the field. He took me under his wing and loved me like a little sister. As I reflect on the instrumental men in my life, he takes the trophy. When we lost our home in a fire, he called his sponsor and got all my ball equipment replaced. He was my refuge in every way. When I think of the ideal patriarchal pillar, it's him I see. Thank you, buddy. You are one of the greats. I know you are pitching risers in heaven and looking down on me with pride. You are the man, the myth, the legend.

In Loving Memory
Rob Scheller
1963-2021

CHAPTER

10

CAPTAIN COMMUNICATOR

CAPTAIN OF YOUR OWN SHIP

*T*hroughout these chapters, we have learned practical tools and skills on how to effectively communicate with ourselves and others. The desired outcome is to fully grasp we aren't victims of words, actions, and circumstances, but to understand we control the narrative. When we see our triggers with x-ray vision, we become our own superheroes. To recognize both our needs in an encounter and the reasons for our reactions is pure power. Although I am a control freak, I am learning to let go of the need to dominate the situation, and instead I control myself. Discipline and willpower are extremely important in achieving Captain Communicator status. The cornerstone of this authority is built upon being a neutralizer. Might isn't always loud and aggressive. When we can utilize the potency of diffusing the internal bombs, we will become masters of calming the external bombs as well. Everyone wants a kick-ass superpower with lasers, Herculean strength, and flying capabilities, but the ability to defuse physical, emotional, or mental bombs is king of all powers. We enter this portal of strength when we achieve magnificent freedom in the uncontrollable. We decide the narrative and when we have the wisdom of this, we can change the narrative. The two go hand-in-hand. From there we get our wings. This status solidifies our abilities to process, translate, recalibrate, and reconcile information at the speed of light. Each day in which we commit to being a captain, we get wiser, faster, and stronger. Living with this intention is key to leaving an impactful legacy for the next generation.

Self-Reflection is necessary. We cannot fully step into our superhero status if we aren't willing to face the truth. We must ask ourselves daily if we are buying into our own fantasy fiction drama or if it's a true story. Turn the mirror on yourself and look at all your wounds and the triggers that mask them. Be gentle with yourself and choose curiosity over criticism. Really get to know how you communicate and what your needs are. How do you best receive and how can you better deliver signals? When we know the five Ws of ourselves (Who, What, When, Where, Why), we discover how we operate. Knowledge is Power,[1] so let's forge our strength by getting to know ourselves. When we truly know something, we develop compassion. Our benevolence is a mighty weapon. It can solve the identity crisis. It can interpret different languages. It can build bridges. It can instill peace. It can heal humanity. It can bring people back to a shared reality. It can transcend time. It can heal the past and reshape our future. It inspires. It perpetuates a sense of purpose. In essence, seeing ourselves and others through a lens of love will unlock the mysteries of human behaviour. There's no more code to crack when we become friends with the mirror. Is the mirror your rival or your refuge? The choice is yours.

Another component of ensuring free-flowing pathways of communication is mastering the art of the pause. I know I've mentioned this before, but I want to recap the power of the five-second rule. Take time to do those deep belly breaths and respond consciously instead of reacting instinctively. The power of the pause puts you back in control of your narrative. When we live in the instant-reactor zone, we are at the mercy of others. They control our responses and play us like a fiddle. I don't want someone else to rule my emotions, my mental state, or my narrative. We are the captains of our own ships but that means we must grasp the controls and navigate the course. When we pause, we calm our nervous system so we can critically think, reconcile information, focus, and calculate an uncharged response. In the pause, we become the neutralizer. If we immediately respond with no breath, inner dialogue, or self-reflection, we become victims to our own triggers.

Just by giving our responses space and time, we get promoted to Captain Communicator status. This is a sign of a true leader. I wrestle with this, but I am devoted to the practice of pausing. Giving an interaction a few extra seconds is a wonderful present to all parties involved. We often feel like we need to provide an instant response, but the more distance and consideration we can place in between comments, the better the conversation. The transmissions will have gone through an incredible refining process. Pausing is another superpower.

We can't be the captain if we don't maintain our boundaries. Building and protecting personal boundaries supports how we drive the narrative and in turn transform the narrative. I was a horrible boundary defender all throughout my life. Everyone was welcome to trample all over me which left me feeling so violated. I was a victim of my own lack of self-respect. I wish someone had told me earlier that I wasn't required to have an open-door policy for others to hurt my heart. If someone is being disrespectful, you don't have to take it. You don't retaliate, but you simply get up and walk away with grace. This demonstrates that a line has been crossed and that you regard yourself with the utmost dignity, love, and admiration. Protecting one's own boundaries and respecting others' are the marks of a true captain. For some reason we rarely express that someone has trespassed our borders, but we should start being that direct. When you really pay attention though, people do indirectly give us hints. Their demeanor shifts or the energy turns cold. People's posture might be in defense mode, and they might just shut down. We need to begin tuning into those frequencies if we want to be better communicators. If we want someone to value our boundaries, we had better be ready to uphold theirs.

If you are looking to be a boundary badass, I suggest learning where the lines are for you and what has to happen to consider them being crossed. This helps us identify the "why" in the trigger moment. For me, my biggest ones are when I feel disrespected, belittled, rejected, or minimized. Those are hard limits for me and when trespassing occurs, I have some phrases I go to so I can clearly articulate that my personal parameters have been infringed upon. Here are some boundary-setting sentences to stop an invasion:

"I can't do that, but I can try to find someone who can."

"I appreciate the gesture, but in the future, I'd prefer..."

"I can't take on any additional responsibilities right now."

"This conversation is making me feel unsafe."

"I'm not comfortable discussing this topic with you."

"I'm sharing this with you not for permission, but to ask for your support."

"Thanks for your concern, but I am happy with my decision and I can handle this."

"I can't attend, but I appreciate the invitation."

"I don't give you permission to do (X) to me."

"I can't do (X), but I'm open to trying (Y)."

"I don't feel safe, so I'm going to remove myself."

"I won't be spoken to in that manner."

"I'm allowed to change my mind and voice my needs."

"Thanks, but I'm not interested."

"I don't feel you are hearing me."

"No thank you."

"No."

It is our birthright to have, protect, and voice our boundaries just as we do when we are in our homes. Our personal space is a version of our homes. Feelings of guilt can arise when we first start to draw boundaries and practice self-care after a lifetime of people-pleasing. People will not always respect your position and may try to make you feel selfish or like the villain. Do not fall into the gaslighting trap. Ignore their tantrums and their fear responses, and hold the line.

LEARN, GROW, & ADJUST COURSE

Never stop learning and acquiring navigation tools. Continually adapt and improve communication skills. This includes being courageous in conflict. Healed and happy people don't hurt others. If we want to act with maturity and maintain growth and healing, then we must ensure our responses to stimuli reflect those missions. A sign someone is hurting from internal wounds and traumas is when they lash out and try to hurt another. Therefore, when we find ourselves wanting to trigger-respond to a personal attack, we are dealing with someone who is deeply hurting inside. This doesn't mean we must accept abuse. We honour our set boundary and walk away with grace. Our innate reaction might be to fire back with a hurtful comment or to withhold our love and empathy. But those aggressors need our compassion the most. We learn when we are willing and humble. Let's commit to healing our wounds instead of hitting back with zingers. We won't grow if we avoid, deflect, or re-wound the wounded.

So, what does lashing out look like?

Cussing at people

Invalidating another's feelings

Attacking another's character

Mocking

Trumpeting that you are more popular or more qualified

Exploiting someone's weaknesses

Bringing others into the fight and creating a pack of wolves' war of words

Deflecting and shaming

Manufacturing false claims about someone

Questioning another's expertise or
credentials

Gaslighting

Being passive-aggressive by "liking" social
media posts that attack other people

Bullying

We can completely disagree with and question views, perspectives, and opinions without attacking the person. Once we go in for the kill, we highlight our own shortcomings. By learning the clues of ourselves and others, we automatically grow in emotional intelligence. And when we mix quality intel with a calm and controlled nervous system, we have the tools and ability to adjust our route in the conversation. We encourage things to de-escalate and neutralize as our brain creates pathways to better send and receive information. This goes back to our responsibilities as the captain of the ship. When there are winds, storms, currents, and other factors at play, we must take the lead and change the course of our conversations.

Conflict, difference of opinions, and disagreements are part of our every day lives, but for some reason we suck at resolving them. Often, we incorporate our views into our identity, and when someone challenges those ideals, we feel like our identity is being attacked. However, conflict and tough talks are actually gifts. The more we can shift our perspective to welcome these dialogues, the better we get at effectively navigating through them. We often hear about conflict resolution but to attain a solution, we must face the conflict. For most of my life I avoided the difficult conversations. My entire body would enter panic-attack mode and my nervous system would send jumbled signals on how to get out of this perceived threat as soon as possible. I always fled. I refused to ever face the uncomfortable exchange. Conflict is unpredictable and scary as hell. As a girl who wanted to control everything, this didn't bode well. But when I finally decided to push through the fear and face the dispute, I found resolution even if it was not necessarily what I had hoped for. When we avoid, we never get closure, and it keeps the discord alive as though we are stuck in purgatory.

Disputes aren't fun but they are the best teachers. The more we create safety in the discrepancies, the quicker we can move through them and reach peace. Conflict isn't as scary as we make it out to be. When we avoid, we give time and space to create false narratives and build up assumptions, anger, anxiety, and resentment. This creates mountains out of molehills.

Fred Rogers, affectionately known as Mr. Rogers, is famous for saying "Anything that's human is mentionable, and anything that is mentionable can be more manageable. When we can talk about our feelings, they become less overwhelming, less upsetting, and less scary."[2] If we can't talk about it, we guarantee communication breakdowns. We don't learn and grow or find a solution. It's a missed opportunity. The biggest lesson I am learning is how to enter controversy with courage and curiosity. Merely entering the encounter with an open mind provides pathways for a shared reality with the person staring back at me. It's hard but a beautiful learning tool. I no longer run away from the clash; instead I lean in with composure.

Being a student of life and diligently honing our skills increases the tools available to us as we process signals. The continued commitment to gather and reconcile information is the cornerstone of growth. Sometimes we need more knowledge before we can proceed with an opinion or action. The jury can still be out while we collect this data. It's okay and safe to stay the decision since a delayed conclusion is better than a hasty one. When people make rash assumptions, their lazy and often faulty reasoning is based on insufficient or incomplete facts. People tend to jump to conclusions because our cognitive system depends on mental timesavers called heuristics, which increase the speed of our assessments and decisions. Unfortunately, the cost is a reduction of accuracy and rationality. Sometimes we misuse certain heuristics, which triggers us to take excessive mental shortcuts. We then jump to unsubstantiated conclusions. To counterbalance premature conclusions, we must weigh our thoughts, all the facts, and every circumstance at play.

I find it funny that we are a culture obsessed with our physical weight, but we rarely weigh our opinions and beliefs. We should care less about our body weight and focus more on weighing information. By design, humans are always looking to cut corners. I'll admit even after all my learning and growing, I still find myself trying to save time and I come up with a baseless narrative. Our brains don't like loose ends; we want an instant and clear-cut answer. However, we must be more truth conscious than body conscious. Weigh the biases and opinions against facts or the spirit of humanity. Could you imagine the positive impact that would ensue? By taking the time to develop our IQ (intelligence quotient), we expand our EQ (emotional quotient, or emotional intelligence). We don't need to rush to an unsupported position. Being neutral until we have enough quality facts to offer an opinion is powerful. And the ultimate indication of growth is discovering that we are open to changing our mind when presented with information that contradicts our original findings.

This brings us to the tipping point where we can co-exist with all these signals and navigate through our life as the hero and not the victim. When we can recalibrate our thoughts, words, and actions in real time, we find better coordinates and adjust our course. We also need to be comfortable with trial and error. Sometimes we take a detour to avoid a collision but end up on a path filled with its own set of roadblocks. That's just part of life, and testing our wisdom and determination against the issues that arise is another superpower. This helps us form effective strategies for ourselves and for others in the communication bubble. Even though I think of myself as a strong student of communication, I still say and do the wrong things. But my batting average is fairly good. When I strike out and completely blow it, I learn and I'm getting quicker at realizing where I missed the mark. I get back on track.

Communication is about finding the right frequency. Many factors in a moment can cause a fuzzy signal, so continue the pursuit of plugging in and fine-tuning the sound. When we get good at picking up the slightest disruption, we can adjust the dial and keep the lines clear for positive sent and received transmissions. Always have your hand on the dial.

UNIVERSAL LANGUAGE

Despite all the languages and dialects spoken throughout the world, there is one that is universally understood: love. This unconditional, intelligent, multi-dimensional, fierce, and mighty attribute is the universal approach to communicating with the eight billion people in this world. Love defies all logic. Love disarms. Love sparks peace treaties. Love disrupts chaos. Love calms inner and outer worlds. Love alters the atmosphere. A drop of love is understood without even one word spoken. It is the cornerstone of deciphering and communicating signals. We don't need to complicate the comms; we just need to commit to leading with love.

I issue a charge today and champion taking up the torch of love. When we learn to love ourselves and see others through the lens of love, we become the universal interpreter. When we get to this juncture, we obtain our captain wings. This isn't about rank, prestige or power, it's about emotional intelligence. EQ is a gift for yourself and the world. To be a Captain Communicator means we have entered a space of clarity and calm where we can observe and absorb information and redirect all intel into signals that neutralize or heal instead of further hurt and disconnect.

This universal language is the bridge. Can you imagine travelling the world and being able to communicate with anyone because we all embody the love language? Pledge your allegiance to love. Love is the heart of all communication, but there are channels that connect and support the love factor. Just like a human heart, love needs arteries and veins to transport and communicate. Decoding and directing self-discipline are the conduits to being a universal translator and communicator. To decode, we enter a neutral space of observation and discernment, and avoid adopting prejudices or early conclusions. It is central to understanding what is happening in our minds and souls as well as in the people and situations we face. If we don't reconcile information from an unbiased space, we cannot trust our verdicts. We either feel overwhelmed by the data and it clogs our systems, or we subconsciously only accept the information that supports our biases in an effort to streamline the data dump. Neither is healthy or effective. We become defective, rather than intelligent, communicators.

Next is self-discipline. We could be great at observing and processing, but it's what we do with the information that matters. Even if we know the answer and it has passed the scale tests, it's our delivery of that information that counts. We might have powerful knowledge to deliver, but understanding how to control the flow of our communication is key. Is it too much or too little? If we don't install the restraint filter, we become kryptonite instead of a healing superpower. Willpower is a superpower. When in doubt, err on the side of love. The willpower superpower is when we choose love over being right. We often don't have all the information or see the entire picture, so let's just love instead of judge. This language is understood all over the world. When I get caught off guard and I'm not sure how to respond to someone hurting me I just reply with "I hear you and thank you for sharing." I don't respond with love and appreciation for being hurt, but my love for myself overrides the urge to hurt back. That simple response is the neutralizer. Don't get me wrong, it's incredibly difficult to do. Self-control is one of the hardest things to master, but is the marker of pure power. When you see someone with superhuman willpower, you know they have gone through advanced training and some serious hellfire to get there. Always do a self-assessment before responding or relaying information. Just taking a pause to reflect and decipher what is ours and theirs and responding from a place of emotional intelligence sets up authentic and loving communication. This ensures people will receive our responses as intended and not through their own fictitious plot. Don't ever let ego win. It's a constant inner battle, but submitting to love guarantees everyone wins.

To communicate universally means to be committed to reaching for reconciliation not confrontation. Some people feed off the feud because it is familiar to them, but in doing so they ensure constant war and disconnect. We must lead with a "peace on purpose" mentality. It's not easy or natural to fight for peace. Humans are instinctively hard-wired to fight and destroy. This might have been the key to our survival at one point long ago, but we must evolve. If the entire world is divided and we are horrible communicators, how do we bridge that? We change our approach and make peace. Let's shift the goal from winning to uniting. Our words can cause wars or end them. Signing a contract within perpetuates peace wherever we go. We can't be a Captain Communicator if we don't liberate our language. Be a peacemaker and construct new pathways of human connection. Let's lead the way for our children to have peace instead of mental-health wars, racism, oppression, abuse, and destruction. To make a better world for our children's tomorrow, we must establish peace within our world today. I connect to all because I let love and peace lead the way. I relinquish my ego and my desire to conquer. Communication isn't about dominance, it's about learning, appreciating, empathising, and sharing a human experience. If we could approach our comms as a way to come away with a better understanding of others and concepts, we would tap into the most renewable source of energy and human sustainability there is—connection.

SIGNAL SUPERPOWER

Our ability to connect with one another depends on our willingness to be vulnerable. Being real, flawed, authentic, genuine, pliable, honest, and exposed are the real superpowers. When we can find power in those qualities, we become the hero. It's the fear, masks, fake perfection, aliases, false identities, and ego that eat away at our true identity and ultimately at our power. I was powerless until I made a resolute decision within myself to just be me. It hasn't been easy. In fact, it's been the hardest thing I've ever done. There are hundreds of voices each day telling us we are not good enough or we are wrong and bad for who we are as we are. My comms systems were all a mess. As I've slowly worked towards establishing new lines and healthy signals again, I realized they led me to the importance of vulnerability. When

I'm vulnerable, I disarm the discord. When I'm vulnerable, I get into a place of acceptance. When I'm vulnerable, I can detect vulnerability in others. When I'm vulnerable, I gain intelligence. Vulnerability activates connection. This all strengthens my input and output of signals.

If you only have one takeaway from this book, please let it be the healing power of vulnerability. I was scared to tell this story. For a year I had panic attacks and rehearsed mock conversations with my parents. This book was never about shock and awe to pump sales, it was all about finding freedom in the fear. I know the only way to unlock the healing of this deadly disease is to be transparent and release all my trauma, shame, and angst. I don't want to die. I have more things to do on this earth to fulfill my destiny and leave my mark on this world. I refuse to leave my daughter without a mother because I was too afraid of vulnerability. Our connection, healing, sovereignty, and super identity are unearthed when we choose courageous honesty.

There will be times when you lead with brave vulnerability and the person staring back at you armours up and shuts you out. It's not you, but it's not just them either. These situations are learning opportunities for both. When you show up authentically and from a heart space, their actions are not your responsibility or problem, but how you respond to them is. I always conclude that in this dance of shame, judgment, trauma, and drama, it's a mix of both of us. When we evolve into a Captain Communicator, we get to be remarkable detectives. I'm amazed at how aware I am now when I'm triggered and at what my emotional, physical, and mental tells are. Some of these triggers may never go away, but I've mastered the detection and awareness of them, and I've sped up the process on how to move through them in a superhero way. This has paved the way to make peace with myself and with others. The devastation from other people's reactions, betrayal, and criticisms were daggers to my heart. But now I'm able to shift the lens, enter a shared reality, and apply grace. My awareness of my own triggers brings into focus the others'. When humans are triggered, they put out a distress signal for their superhero to come rescue them. When we become a Captain Communicator, we can rescue ourselves and even assist others by diffusing the charge.

The more we know, the more we grow. We build mental muscles and therefore increase our power. Even after achieving superhero status, we aren't done yet though. We must keep knowing and growing. There's always more to uncover and more to learn on a deeper level. Sometimes we think we have mastered a concept or a strategy but there are layers to this process, and we can always press in for more profound knowledge. I am addicted to learning how to communicate with my body and soul. This commitment has changed the trajectory of my life and even saved it. I was the walking dead, and my body would've followed suit if I hadn't faced the wound to find the light. The might that comes with an iron will to live is the greatest feeling in the world. I have been through hell and back, but this means I am fashioned in the fire. When we can look at all our hardships and circumstances that burned our promises, dreams, and hopes, and stand on the ashes with gratitude, wisdom, and a hungry spirit, we become the superpower.

Every day and in every way, we can heal and strengthen our signals. Even when there's nothing left to repair, we can build new roads with wiser and kinder intelligence. No longer do we need to conquer others to elevate ourselves. When we champion ourselves and support humanity, we become victorious. Swearing an oath to knowing and growing is a power that can never be subdued. Daily, we are faced with choices on whether to show up authentically or with an alias. We must assume the mantle of realistic representation. Imperfect authenticity triumphs over false identity. It is safe to be you. It is safe to be me. Our aliases and armour are the kryptonite. We cannot decode and harness the beautiful power of our signals if we coat them with viruses and fake perfection. Taking all these nuggets of wisdom and applying them to our everyday lives will clear a path for us to own our lives rather than be passenger in them. We are not slaves to our trauma. We are not prisoners of our past. We are stronger because of them. Let's harness all our hardships and allow them to be the secret intelligence that propels us into our purpose. In every signal that we face, we have the opportunity to let the hardships empower our vulnerability and shape our super identity. If we don't, we grant them access to hurt and hide us. We mustn't cower.

I am sounding the alarm. Our lives and the lives of future generations all depend on us answering the call of courage. Don't mask up, but reveal the exquisite superhero you are. Turn all your pain into passion. Shed all the shame and labels and take on the label of Captain Communicator. We are the answer we have been crying out for. Be present and be seen. Our true identity is our super identity. Nothing can stop us when we are marching together with our unique assignments. Can you hear the roars of people? Can you see the beautiful hearts all knowing they are enough and are the captains of their souls? Can you envision what kind of humanity that would look like? A crescendo of valour. Billions of Captain Communicators moving as one.

EPILOGUE

PROVOKED INTO PURPOSE

"If it doesn't challenge you; it doesn't
change you" – Fred DeVito.[1]

When humanity transforms our view on the challenges we face, we will discover our unique purpose. There will never be a pearl without pain. I dedicate this book to all the pains I have encountered. Not because of petty spite, but because they pushed me to where I am supposed to be. The taunts from tragedies are gifts. Often, we don't view them this way, so we run or resist. The misery is our muse. For years I ran from this illness. I camouflaged the rejection and hurt. I repelled the tough lessons, and my life embodied the rejection. Fear paralyzed me. I went through life frozen and stagnant. The pain was familiar and therefore comfortable. Stepping out was unknown and scary. I was a victim of the torments rather than the victor. When I came to the realization that they were the key to unlocking my purpose, I found meaning to my life. Those people, circumstances, and trauma were not there to end me, they were there to lead me.

This book is a deliberate provocation to trigger us forward. Communication is connection. We must connect to the nemesis and let it propel us into growth. When we grow, we evolve. When we evolve, we become wise. When wisdom and maturity collide, we encounter purpose. I was drowning in my gasps for air and in heart-wrenching grief. When you fight for your life and you must will yourself to breathe to stay alive, there are moments you contemplate your very existence. Is this my life? Is this how my story ends? So many of us struggle to survive, and yet we choose the familiar agony over the foreign fear. I encourage you to face whatever you are fighting right now. Use the force against you to thrust you forward. Stop marrying the mediocrity. This is not where our destinies lay. There is more to our lives than the pain. The pearl is outside of our comfort zone. When we build a highly sophisticated and emotionally intelligent comms system within, we construct the confidence to fight for our lives. When we see those traumas as potential pearls, we can shout CHARGE! Do not shy away from the sword. Do not yield. See the hardships with new eyes and welcome them.

I am healing every time I press into the problem. I am still working out total restoration, but I look back on the last seven years of my life and I see a string of pearls assembled by all my pain. Some trials are more difficult than others, but they are all an opportunity to take a step closer to my purpose. So, the next time your trauma response pops up, identify how your previous self wanted to cope.

Flight: workaholic, anxious, obsessive-compulsive, restless, perfectionist, and sad.

Fight: raging, controlling, bullying, judging, or self-harming.

Freeze: indecisive, stuck, numb, shut down, isolated, exhausted, and mentally checked out.

Fawn: people-pleasing, unable to uphold personal boundaries, overwhelmed, lack of identity, codependent, and self-critical.

Do the opposite. Don't fall into the trigger trap. Face the fear/trauma and let it fuel you towards your purpose instead of away from it. We control the narrative of our lives. We have the tools to communicate and process. We are the captains of the ship. Decode the difficulties and choose life. Our challenges are there to champion us into our destiny. This acceptance is the key to disarming the rejection. Walking in our purpose is our superpower, for purpose connects us in all realms of communication. We are Captain Communicators.

ABOUT THE AUTHOR

Blaise Hunter is breaking barriers with her consulting agency, Blaise the Trail Inc. Known as the Modern-Day Superhero–Heroine, she contends for women to own their super identity.

Blaise is an author, multi-award-winning humanitarian, international speaker, fertility expert, certified human rights advocate, copywriter, Mother of Purpose, and Breaker of Chains. Blaise is on a crusade to fight for social justice, specializing in women's reproductive health rights. After experiencing three miscarriages of her own, she founded the non-profit group Footprints: Infertility & Pregnancy Loss Support Initiative which is changing the medical system one hospital at a time. She shatters the veil of silence and inspires women to pick up their miscarried dreams and be Mothers of Purpose. She is the multi-faceted CEO who helps people birth their identity, voices, dreams, rights, books, and brands. Blaise is the fertility expert who doesn't help people get pregnant, but who empowers them to be fertile in their lives and expectant with purpose, and to breathe fire.

Blaise offers advice and expertise to people and organizations to help them improve their business performance in terms of brand identity and marketing strategy. She also helps clients write their books and compose their keynote speeches. Blaise draws from years of experience in broadcast journalism, public relations, and entrepreneurship. She is an award-winning writer who brilliantly combines her wit with her flare. She helps clients "Leverage their Brand Language" with creative copywriting. Blaise is a freelance writer turned multi-hyphenate CEO who loves showing purpose-driven entrepreneurs how to harness the power of content marketing. Through her trademark "strategic storytelling" approach to copywriting and content creation, Blaise helps creatives, coaches, and founders become go-to experts in their industry as they launch impactful offerings that grow their audiences.

Blaise founded the award-winning non-profit organization Footprints: Infertility & Pregnancy Loss Support Initiative to help heal her heart and a broken system. She is leading the charge to break the silent barriers around this issue and cause an empathy outbreak. No longer do we need to feel ashamed or sit alone with our pain. Blaise is in the business of hope. Hope drives change. Hope provokes peace. Hope heals humanity. If we can harness hope, we can heal parents' hearts and make our angel babies count. The mandate for Footprints is a two-part mission.

1. Improve the systems on the frontlines to ensure parents get the proper care, information, and emotional support the moment their trauma happens. This includes giving out handmade mental health support bags worldwide and working with medical establishments, governing bodies, and workplaces

to implement better protocols and procedures when handling infertility, miscarriages, and stillbirths.

2. Create a universal support community to continue the efforts in bridging the gap in care for emotional and mental health in the weeks, months, and years following a loss.

Blaise champions the next generation by teaching them to Know Their Worth through her youth mental health outreach. She empowers youth to draw their swords and breathe fire as she speaks on stages around the world at education and mental health conferences. Blaise is a sought-after advocate for social programming with topics of body positivity, confidence, purpose, and changing the narrative.

Blaise lives with her husband and daughter in Nanaimo, British Columbia. Her family is her greatest achievement of all.

Blaise the Trail inc.

Blaise HUNTER ®

REVIEWS

Blaise Hunter is an extraordinary writer, speaker, and humanitarian. She advocates for change, healing, and creating a better, safer world. Through her writing and speaking, she is always provoking people to think, listen, and relearn. She does this by asking questions, providing truth to her stories, and being authentic. She is always taking people on a journey through her storytelling to show that change and healing are both possible and essential to living your life to the fullest. Not only does she provide an opportunity for readers to get to know her, but she provides a space for people to map out their own story, and she inspires the world to be better as a whole. All of Blaise Hunter's writing is powerful and thought-provoking. Her books and her articles are a must read.

~ Krista Malden, CEO & Publisher of
Community Now! Magazine

Blaise is a gem to work with. She was referred to me by a friend, and after our first consultation call, I knew she would be the perfect fit to help me build my brand and website. Blaise has a way with words, and she has a gift of capturing exactly what you envision. She is easy to work with and is driven to help you achieve your goals within your business.

She was always so prompt in her delivery to me and always open to making any changes or revisions to make sure I got exactly what I was looking for. I highly recommend Blaise and her skills and services. She took a huge weight off my plate which allowed me to focus on the passion of my work with ease and grace.

~ Anne-Marie Evans, *The Erotic Spirit*

Blaise is a master at illustrating the emotions we all face and showing the strength behind them. She is a talented writer.

~ Amazon customer

When experiencing Blaise speak on stage, it's like watching a theatrical performance. She has a rare gift to hold the energy of the room and pull raw emotion from the crowd. I love her analogies and her fire.

~ Audience member

The Footprints: Infertility & Pregnancy Loss Support Initiative is especially important to my husband and me. After suffering three miscarriages, we were sent home with very little to no information and a whirlwind of emotions. Not understanding how to deal with the emotions can really feel like you are the only ones suffering. What Blaise has done for reproductive health rights is remarkable. We went to the Footprints meeting and received an information package from her. It was full of support and empathy, and I believe everyone should get that chance to feel supported and not alone in trauma and suffering.

~Teresa

Blaise is a fearless advocate for infertility and pregnancy loss and has a true talent in making her words just as striking as her actions with writing that is impactful, grounded, and strong. Blaise knows the true power of words and honours that in everything she writes, writing with a passion and with purpose. Congratulations on this latest book Blaise; I'm certain it will make waves.

~ Olivia Flavell, Researcher and Co-Founder
of the Greco-Northern Research Hub.

If you are interested in working with Blaise or having her speak at your next event, contact her today. Let us Breathe Fire together.

BlaiseHunter.com
Social Media Handle - @blaisethetrail

LEARN HOW TO RISE UP AS YOUR OWN HEROINE

FINALIST AT THE CANADIAN BOOK CLUB AWARDS

Five Stars!!!

Heroine by Blaise Hunter provides a candid and authentic view of challenges facing women today. As a mental health professional, a woman, and a mother I recommend this book. The author shares her own experiences with challenging topics including self-image, fertility, and parenting in a humorous and relatable fashion. Through her narrative, Blaise and the women featured in this book validate women's shared life experiences in trying to live up to the image of being a perfect wife, ever-doting mother, and successful career woman all at once. This book shows the reader how to recognize and reframe some of the negative thoughts that arise from comparing our own "behind the scenes footage" to other women's "highlight reels" as are most often portrayed on social media. Themes of self-discovery, self-compassion, and self-acceptance are underpinned in every chapter. Hunter provides useful insights to challenge social norms, negative self-talk, and to promote self-care. This book focuses on helping women to learn to live their lives with passion and fire. ~ Michelle

Order Today
BlaiseHunter.com

NOTES

CHAPTER 1 - KNOW THYSELF

[1]	Wikipedia, "Know Thyself" (Last modified June 26, 2022). https://en.wikipedia.org/wiki/Know_thyself

[2]	Val Snow, "The causes of disease in ourselves: why people get sick," *Healthy Food Near Me* (Nov 6, 2021). https://healthy-food-near-me.com/the-causes-of-disease-in-ourselves-why-people-get-sick/

[3]	University of California - Los Angeles, "Study shows how serotonin and a popular anti-depressant affect the gut's microbiota" *ScienceDaily* (Sept 6, 2019). www.sciencedaily.com/releases/2019/09/190906092809.htm

[4]	Esther and John Veltheim, "Stress Disorders" (PDF) (February 20, 2018). https://www.bodytalksystem.com/assets/books/Stress.Disorders.pdf

CHAPTER 2 - LIVING MY RELIGION

[1]	I have received the following training and certifications:
MindScape course. IBA Global Healing, with Chantelle Rogers. 2015
Chakradance Instructor Certification, with founder Natalie Southgate. 2015
FreeFall 1 course. IBA Global Healing, with Allison Bachmeier. 2016
Joan Hunter, *Healing Starts Now! Complete Training Manual.* (Shippensburg, PA: Destiny Image® Publishers, Inc., 2013). Completed study in 2016

The Soul's Journey Exploring the Mind and the Three Brains. IBA Global Healing, with founder Dr. John Veltheim. 2017

FreeFall 2 course. IBA Global Healing, with Allison Bachmeier. 2017

Dr. Caroline Leaf, *Switch on Your Brain* curriculum DVD and workbook (Grand Rapids, MI: Baker Books, 2015). Completed study in 2018

[2] Lisa Bevere, "The Church's Autoimmune Disease" on LIFE Today (aired June 28, 2022). 2'10." https://www.youtube.com/watch?v=UfbnwGcwpYY

CHAPTER 3 - COUPLE CONVERSATIONS

[1] Tony Robbins, "Types of Communication Styles" (accessed July 3, 2022). https://www.tonyrobbins.com/personal-growth/communication-styles/

[2] Brené Brown, host, with Dr. Harriet Lerner, "I'm Sorry: How to Apologize and Why It Matters Part 1" *Unlocking Us* (podcast) (May 6, 2020). https://brenebrown.com/podcast/harriet-lerner-and-brene-i m-sorry-how-to-apologize-why-it-matters-part-1-of-2/

[3] Brené Brown, host, with Dr. Harriet Lerner, "I'm Sorry: How to Apologize and Why It Matters Part 2" *Unlocking Us* (podcast) (May 8, 2020). https://brenebrown.com/podcast/im-sorry-how-t o-apologize-why-it-matters-part-2-of-2/

[4] Katie Evans and J. Michael Sullivan. *Treating Addicted Survivors of Trauma*. New York: Guilford Press, 1995. Quote Page 147. (accessed Sept 3, 2022). Google Book Search.

CHAPTER 4 - MINI-ME

[1] Mother Teresa, Acceptance Speech, The Noble Peace Prize 1979, Nobel Prize Outreach AB 2022 (accessed Sept 3, 2022). https://www.nobelprize.org/prizes/peace/1979/teresa/acceptance-speech/

[2] Benjamin Franklin. "Most people die at 25 and aren't buried until 75" (accessed July 13, 2022). https://www.goodreads.com/quote s/85334-many-people-die-at-twenty-five-and-aren-t-buried-until

CHAPTER 6 - THE 'RENTS

1   Rumi, "The wound is the place where the Light enters you" (accessed July 20, 2022). https://www.goodreads.com/quotes/103315-the-woun d-is-the-place-where-the-light-enters-you

2   Dr. Phil McGraw, "We teach people how to treat us" (accessed July 20, 2022). https://www.goodreads.com/quotes/196112-we-teac h-people-how-to-treat-us

3   Alexandra definition, "defender/protector of man" and the "one who saves warriors" Baby name finder. (accessed July 20, 2022). https:// mom.com/baby-names/girl/18951/Alexandra

4   Eren, "10 fascinating facts about REM sleep" Facty Health (January 28, 2021). https://facty.com/anatomy/brain-anatomy/10-fascinating-facts-about-rem-sleep/

CHAPTER 7 - OFFICE SPACE

1   Desmond Tutu, "There comes a point where we need to stop just pulling people out of the river. We need to go upstream and find out why they're falling in." (accessed July 22, 2022). https://www. goodreads.com/quotes/954454-there-comes-a-point-where-we-n eed-to-stop-just

2   United Nations, "The Universal Declaration of Human Rights" (December 10, 1948. Accessed July 22, 2022). https://www.un.org/ en/about-us/universal-declaration-of-human-rights

3   Ibid.

4   FLEET, "Physicists invent flux capacitor, break time-reversal symmetry" Phys Org (May 28, 2018). https://phys.org/news/2018-0 5-physicists-flux-capacitor-time-reversal-symmetry.html

5   Kenneth Branagh, Director. Cinderella (2015 American film). Walt Disney Pictures, Kinberg Genre, Allison Shearmur Productions, Beagle Pug Films. March 15, 2015. 106 min. (Have courage and be kind…) https://www.moviequotesandmore.com/cinderella-quotes/

6   Canadian Women's Foundation, "The Facts About the Gender Pay Gap" (March 15, 2022). https://canadianwomen.org/the-facts/ the-gender-pay-gap/

[7] Elise Gould, "Equal Pay Day" Working Economics Blog, Economic Policy Institute (March 10, 2022). https://www.epi.org/blog/equal-pay-day-there-has-been-little-progress-in-closing-the-gender-wage-gap/

[8] Canadian Women's Foundation, "The Facts about the Gender Pay Gap" (March 15, 2022). https://canadianwomen.org/the-facts/the-gender-pay-gap/

[9] Canadian Human Rights Commission, "Pregnancy and Human Rights in the Workplace A Guide for Employers" (PDF) (Ottawa, ON: 2010). https://www.chrc-ccdp.gc.ca/sites/default/files/publication-pdfs/pregnancy_grossesse-eng.pdf

[10] Canadian Human Rights Commission, "Policy on Pregnancy & Human Rights in the Workplace," Pregnancy & Human Rights in the Workplace - Policy and Best Practices, page 1. (January 1, 2011). https://www.chrc-ccdp.gc.ca/en/resources/policy-pregnancy-human-rights-the-workplace-page-1

[11] Jim Wilson, "Does Canada need a bereavement leave for miscarriage?" Canadian HRReporter (March 26, 2021). https://www.hrreporter.com/focus-areas/compensation-and-benefits/does-canada-need-a-bereavement-leave-for-miscarriage/354338

[12] Blaise Hunter, host, "Episode 22 A Culture of Kindness – Blaise Hunter interviews Nahla Summers" Blaise the Trail (podcast) (July 10, 2020). https://businessinnovatorsradio.com/blaise-the-trail-ep-22-a-culture-of-kindness-blaise-hunter-interviews-nahla-summers/

[13] Kim Parker and Juliana Menasce Horowitz, "The Great Resignation: Majority of workers who quit a job in 2021 cite low pay, no opportunities for advancement, feeling disrespected," Pew Research Center, (March 9, 2022). https://www.pewresearch.org/fact-tank/2022/03/09/majority-of-workers-who-quit-a-job-in-2021-cite-low-pay-no-opportunities-for-advancement-feeling-disrespected/

CHAPTER 8 - VENUS

[1] Clarissa Pinkola Estés, "Within every woman there lives a powerful force filled with good instincts, passionate creativity, and ageless knowing. She is the Wild Woman," Blurb for *Women*

Who Run with the Wolves (New York: Ballantine Books, 1992) (accessed July 26, 2022). https://www.clarissapinkolaestes.com/ women_who_run_with_the_wolves__myths_and_stories_of_ the_wild_woman_archetype_101250.htm

2   John Bradshaw, "E-motions are energy in motion. They are the energy that moves us—our human fuel." (accessed July 26, 2022). bukrate.com/author/john-bradshaw-quotes

3   Stephen P. Wickstrom, "Adam's Rib" (Blog) (2021). http://www. spwickstrom.com/rib/

CHAPTER 9 - MARS

1   Alison Armstrong, "Stages of Manhood" (accessed July 27, 2022). https://www.pinterest.ca/pin/513480794995295918/

CHAPTER 10 - CAPTAIN COMMUNICATOR

1   Wikipedia, "*Scientia Potentia Est*/Knowledge is Power" (Last modified July 26, 2022. Accessed July 27, 2022). https://en.wikipedia. org/wiki/Scientia_potentia_est

2   Mr. Fred Rogers, "Anything that's human is mentionable, and anything that is mentionable can be more manageable. When we can talk about our feelings, they become less overwhelming, less upsetting, and less scary." (accessed July 27, 2022). https:// www.goodreads.com/quotes/157666-anything-that-s-human-is-m entionable-and-anything-that-is-mentionable

EPILOGUE - PROVOKED INTO PURPOSE

1   Fred DeVito. "If it doesn't challenge you; it doesn't change you". (accessed July 31, 2022). https://www.goodreads.com/quotes/64663 8-if-it-doesn-t-challenge-you-it-doesn-t-change-you..